Seven Steps to Peace

Seven Steps to Peace

R. PAUL CAUDILL

BROADMAN PRESS
Nashville, Tennessee

© Copyright 1982 • Broadman Press
All rights reserved.

4215-27
ISBN: 0-8054-1527-0

Acknowledgments: All Scripture quotations from the Book of Philippians are taken from R. Paul Caudill, *Philippians: A Translation with Notes* (Boone, NC: Blue Ridge Press of Boone, Inc., 1980).

All Scripture quotations from the Book of Ephesians are taken from R. Paul Caudill, *Ephesians: A Translation with Notes* (Nashville: Broadman Press, 1979).

All Scripture quotations other than from the Book of Philippians and the Book of Ephesians are quoted from the American Standard Version unless otherwise noted.

Quotations marked RSV are from the Revised Standard Version of the Bible, copyrighted 1946, 1952, © 1971, 1973.

Dewey Decimal Classification: 227.6
Subject heading: Bible. N.T. PHILIPPIANS 4:4-9
Library of Congress Catalog Card Number: 81-71254
Printed in the United States of America

*Dedicated to the memory of
my maternal grandfather and grandmother,
George Elihu Myers
and
Mary Elizabeth Staley Myers,
whose righteous lives radiated
God's peace so clearly.*

Preface

During my thirty-one-year pastorate at First Baptist Church, Memphis, Tennessee, as many people with troubled hearts came to me seeking counsel, I found that the key to inner peace lies in the realm of God's Spirit. Case after case could be brought in focus to illustrate this truth. When I was able to lead the person to a closer relationship with Jesus Christ and his teachings, and to a personal understanding of the miraculous transformation Christ can bring about in human personality, I found it possible to lead the individual into a gradual recovery of hope for life and life's true meaning.

In helping to effect this mental transformation, I resorted to the persuasive counsel of the Scriptures and the passage to which I most often turned is found in the fourth chapter of Philippians, verses 4-9.

While the letter to the Philippians is, in a measure, a letter of thanksgiving for the beautiful relationship that existed between Paul and the Philippians, it is also a message of encouragement to a people who were struggling in a sea of troubles. The affluent days of the gold and silver mines were a thing of the past, and many were beggarly poor. They were a people with adversaries (1:28-30), concerning whom Paul gave stern words of warning (3:2). Moreover, the people as a whole must have been desperately in need of compassionate concern from someone who could help them to interpret their problems and aid them in the development of a Christian life-style that would be consistent with their profession as followers of Jesus.

Consequently, Paul, as if in a final burst of praise and confidence, counseled with the Philippians in words (Phil. 4:4-9) that amount to almost an admonitory hymn of praise with the resulting promise of inner peace. So logical and explicit are his words of encouragement, and with such persuasive sequence, that I have chosen to title the passage *Seven Steps to Peace*.

Over the years as a spiritual counselor, I used this passage of Scripture in a continuing effort to enrich the lives of individuals and to aid them in the development of a growing faith and to develop their ability to cope with the frustrating experiences of life that tend to lead to mental depression and fragmented personalities. The apostle Paul, in these words, sought to outline a positive course of thought and action that even the simplest of minds can follow. As in the Beatitudes, there is an ascending progression of thought in the passage. The words are almost as a ladder slanting heavenward. To slowly climb this ladder by faith and with single-hearted devotion to God, one experiences in the end the "peace of God which surpasses all understanding" (4:7). What is more, Paul assured his Philippian friends that this peace of God "shall guard your hearts and your thoughts with Christ Jesus," and that "the God of the peace shall be with you" forever.[1]

Let us now turn and consider Paul's words and how they may become for distracted minds as steps to peace.

R. Paul Caudill

"Ferndale"

Contents

Introduction *by Wayne E. Oates* 11
Step 1 *Keep a Joyful Heart* 13
Step 2 *Manifest Sweet Reasonableness* 23
Step 3 *Be Conscious of the Lord's Presence* 33
Step 4 *Avoid Overanxiety* 39
Step 5 *Be Prayerful* 49
Step 6 *Think Good Thoughts* 59
Step 7 *Practice the Gospel* 69
God's Peace 77

Introduction
by Wayne E. Oates

One of my consistent concerns in both preaching and pastoral care has been the wise and compassionate interpretation of the Scriptures to facilitate, enrich, and direct the formation of a consistent Christian life-style in the lives of people who seek counsel. Paul Caudill draws on his classical, scholarly education in Bible study, his veteran contact with human beings in crisis, and his considerate approach to life-situation preaching to make my task and your task easier and more accurate as undershepherds of the Great Shepherd, Jesus Christ, Our Lord.

Befitting to his purpose, he has chosen the Epistle of Paul to the Philippians to identify seven steps to the kind of peace that arises from the disciplines of Christian love. He does not give us a sentimental gusher for "keeping a joyful heart." No one that reads Philippians, written as a prison letter, can come away with a Pollyanna "positive mental attitude" fostered by self-reassurance. To the contrary, Pastor Caudill fits the peace to the cost of peace in human suffering for Christ's sake.

The exercises in spiritual self-exploration he suggests at the end of each chapter make reading the Epistle to the Philippians and the examination of your own "roots" an adventure in deep gratitude.

In a day when pop psychology at every hand encourages a kind of narcissism, Pastor Caudill gets at the importance of patient reasonableness that is fostered by the vision of Christ in difficult and trying people. In a day when the raising of consciousness rarely reaches any level except our own vested rights and privilege, this book dares to speak of the consciousness of the Lord's Presence as the source of reverence for all people's burdens as well as our own. In a day when we are prone to think that all anxiety is bad and should be quieted by some chemical hope, Paul Caudill speaks to us of anxiety as a runaway creativity that goes out of control because our values are wrongly focused and our awareness of the comradeship and purpose of God has been deflected and dimmed by lesser values. Then, in a day when meditation is becoming so popular we do not have a clear idea of what it is, Paul Caudill gives meaning and substance to it by calling it what it is for the Christian—prayer. He puts himself in the Philippians' place and exegetes the words of Paul to them about the down-to-earth indispensability of prayer as a constant frame of mind, walk of life, and way of thinking creatively before God in Jesus Christ.

If you read the Epistle to the Philippians and follow it with this fine exegesis, you will find Paul Caudill concluding by getting down to the brass tacks of practicing the Christian faith. The Christian is a person of action—individual and social.

I have found reading this book to be a guide to faith and practice in Jesus Christ as I work in a most intense place of ministry to students caring for persons in all manner of human difficulty. You will, too, wherever you are. You have a treat in store for you. Read on!

Professor of Psychiatry and Behavioral Sciences
Director, Program in Ethics and Pastoral Counseling
University of Louisville School of Medicine
Department of Psychiatry and Behavioral Sciences
Louisville, Kentucky

Step 1
Keep a Joyful Heart

Rejoice in the Lord at all times; again I will say rejoice continually (Phil. 4:4).

If there were ever a person qualified to encourage people to endeavor to keep a joyful heart, it was the apostle Paul. Consider his personal experience as he related it in 2 Corinthians 11:24-33:

> Of the Jews five times received I forty stripes save one. Thrice was I beaten with rods, once was I stoned, thrice I suffered shipwreck, a night and a day have I been in the deep; in journeyings often, in perils of rivers, in perils of robbers, in perils from my countrymen, in perils from the Gentiles, in perils in the city, in perils in the wilderness, in perils in the sea, in perils among false brethren; in labor and travail, in watchings often, in hunger and thirst, in fastings often, in cold and nakedness. Besides those things that are without, there is that which presseth upon me daily, anxiety for all the churches. Who is weak, and I am not weak? Who is caused to stumble, and I burn not? If I must needs glory, I will glory of the things that concern my weakness. The God and Father of the Lord Jesus, he who is blessed for evermore knoweth that I lie not. In Damascus the governor under Aretas the king guarded the city of the Damascenes in order to take me: and through a window was I let down in a basket by the wall, and escaped his hands.[1]

A person is to endeavor to keep a joyful heart at all times, and under all circumstances of life, for the quality of joy is a mark of the child of God which all true believers can share. It is an inner experience that springs from a human-divine relationship such as the apostle Paul enjoyed while in prison and with the certain knowledge that death, at the hands of his enemies, was only a stone's throw away.

The joyful heart does not stem from material affluence, from physical health, from the presence of one's dearest neighbors and friends, or even from the beloved presence of one's own family—one's own flesh and blood. It comes rather from above, even as James said, "Every good gift and every perfect gift is from above, coming down from the Father of lights, with whom can be no variation, neither shadow that is cast by turning" (1:17).

The verb translated *rejoice* is the present active imperative (just as in Phil. 3:1), and Paul repeated the entreaty to keep on rejoicing the second time merely for the sake of emphasis. Remember that he was writing to a people who had known great discouragement, and who were poor so far as this world's goods are concerned. Still they shared in the offerings that Paul was taking in behalf of the poor in the Jerusalem church, and out of their "proof of affliction," said Paul, "the abundance of their joy and their deep poverty abounded unto the riches of their liberality. For according to their power, I bear witness, yea and beyond their power, they gave of their own accord" (2 Cor. 8:2-3). In fact, the Philippians were in such poor financial circumstances that Paul seemed reluctant to receive their gifts, for he spoke of their "beseeching us with much entreaty in regard of this grace, and the fellowship in the ministering to the saints" (8:4).

Let us also observe that the kind of rejoicing of which the apostle Paul spoke is rejoicing "in the Lord." Many of us are perhaps disposed to feel that we can rejoice only when things are going well—only when "the lines are fallen unto me in pleasant places," as the psalmist said (16:6). The human side of us is disposed to feel that there is joy for us only when everything turns to our favor.

Now and then one comes upon those who have never

experienced the type of frustrations, disappointments, and sorrow that attend the lives of many people in today's world. Such persons have never lost a loved one; they have never known infidelity to the marriage bond; they have never had a son or a daughter to go astray by deviating from the commonly accepted standards of morality; they have had no business reverses; they have always been able to pay their bills promptly and to see something neatly laid away for the rainy day. Somehow when a person like that counsels you "to look up," "to have faith," and "to pray believingly," the words do not have quite the same ring of the words of one who has passed through the fire, like Paul.

When one comes to experience the relationship of which Jesus spoke in John 15:7 ("If ye abide in me, and my words abide in you, ask whatsoever ye will, and it shall be done unto you"), there is an altogether different basis of perspective, an altogether new standard of evaluation. For then one begins to think not so much in terms of the present life and the things that have to do with one's daily fare but rather upon the life that is to come—the life that is to be realized in the last day. When one's affections center on earthly things, it is obvious that he has not yet entered into the new life-style which is characteristic of the true children of God and which finds its perfect consummation in the last day.

In speaking of his own trials while in prison, the apostle Paul said to his Ephesian friends, "Therefore I beg you not to lose heart in thinking about my trials in your behalf, which are your glory" (3:13). And to this end he admonished them to speak to themselves "in psalms and hymns and spiritual songs, singing and playing on the harp in your heart to the Lord, giving thanks at all times in behalf of everything in the name of our Lord Jesus Christ to the God and Father" (Eph. 5:19-20).[2]

After all, as Paul said so beautifully in Romans 8:18, "The sufferings of this present time are not worthy to be compared with the glory which shall be revealed to us-ward."

If one has truly come to know the Savior, and is risen with him into the earthly phase of the new life, then he is to set his affection on "the things that are above, not on the things that are upon the earth" (Col. 3:1-3).

In the words of Robert Browning,

> Then, welcome each rebuff
> That turns earth's smoothness rough,
> Each sting that bids nor sit nor stand but go!
> Be our joys three-parts pain!
> Strive, and hold cheap the strain;
> Learn, nor account the pang; dare, never grudge the throe!
> ....
> To man, propose this test—
> Thy body at its best,
> How far can that project thy soul on its lone way?
> ....
> As the bird wings and sings.
> Let us cry, "All good things
> Are ours, nor soul helps flesh more, now, than flesh helps soul!"[3]

For many people, being a nominal follower of Jesus Christ has cost them little or nothing in the trials of circumstance. Girded with affluence and bounty, life has been for them "a lark." They have always been able to go where they would and to fulfill almost every earthly desire. In a word, they have suffered no loss for Christ's sake.

But it was different with the apostle Paul. Hear him speak again:

> But whatever things were gains to me, these I have deliberately regarded as loss because of Christ. Yea rather indeed I still consider all things to be loss because of the surpassing greatness of the personal knowledge of Christ Jesus my Lord, for whose sake I suffered the loss of all things, and regard them as rubbish in order that I might gain Christ, and be found in him, not having my own righteousness that is of the law, but the righteousness that is through faith in Christ, the righteousness of God that is based on the faith, that

> I may come to know him personally and the power of his resurrection and fellowship of his sufferings, being conformed to his death, if somehow I might attain unto the resurrection from the dead (Phil. 3:7-11).

Furthermore, note how Paul concluded his brief autobiographical profile: "But one thing I do, forgetting the things that are behind and stretching myself forward towards the things ahead, I keep pressing on toward the goal for the prize of the upward calling of God in Christ Jesus" (Phil. 3:13b-14). Paul was saying in substance, "I know what I'm saying. I've thought of everything that can possibly happen. And still I say it—Rejoice!"[4]

The source of true joy, I repeat, is not found in things but rather is independent of things. The source of true joy is a vital, continuing relationship with Jesus Christ. It is his presence in the life of the believer that brings both joy and peace. One must be "a lover of the Lord," as the old hymn says; for if one is truly a lover of the Lord and continuously experiences his life-giving presence, then he can be happy wherever he is and in whatever circumstance falls his way. (Read Phil. 4:11.)

A beautiful example of this kind of joy occurred in Memphis when a gifted physician was stricken with a fatal disease. He was my personal physician, and I came to know him intimately during his illness. I was with him at the time of the discovery of the malady which, as of now, is still incurable. I secured reservations for him in a Boston hotel when he went, as an outpatient, to a famous clinic there so that the Memphis diagnosis might be carefully checked. He wanted to be confident, in his own mind, of the certainty of the diagnosis. I was with him again and again in the Memphis hospital where he received more than three hundred transfusions of blood.

One day as I was on the point of leaving his room, he asked me if I had time to tarry a moment longer as he had something very special he wanted to share with me. Naturally I indicated that I had all the time in the world for him and waited for his next word. Presently, he raised up in the bed, swung his frail limbs around to a sitting position on the bed, and motioned for me to come near him. As I drew near, he placed his right hand on my left shoulder and his left hand on my right shoulder and looking me squarely in the eyes said, "Paul, I want you to know that there is no bitterness in my heart about this experience. I have peace with my God, and it is all right!" And then he said, "Perhaps God is working out some purpose in all this. And if it should accomplish his purpose, in this I will find my greatest joy!" I knew very well the point of reference in his last remark. I knew of a loved one that he was hoping his illness might serve to bring to a closer walk with God.

When two people love each other, nothing else really matters too much. If they are happy together, they are happy wherever they are. Even so, the child of God knows that no human situation—no earthly circumstance—can deprive him of the Lord's presence, for the Lord has promised us that he will be with us "always, even unto the end of the world" (Matt. 28:20) if we are faithful in our mission for him in all our ways.

This is not to suggest that there will never be times of hardship, disappointment, ill health, and genuine sorrow in one's life when he is a sincere, devoted follower of Jesus Christ. Just the opposite—for Jesus said, "Blessed are they that have been persecuted for righteousness' sake: for theirs is the kingdom of heaven. Blessed are ye when men shall reproach you, and persecute you, and say all manner of evil against you falsely, for my sake. Rejoice, and be exceeding glad: for great is your reward in heaven: for so persecuted they the prophets that were before you" (Matt. 5:10-12). "If the world hateth you," said Jesus, "ye know that it hath hated me before it hated you. If ye were of the world, the world would love its own: but because ye are not of the world, but I chose you out of the world, therefore the world hateth you" (John 15:18-19).

Step 1

> God hath not promised skies always blue,
> Flower-strewn pathways, all our lives through;
> God hath not promised sun without rain,
> Joy without sorrow, peace without pain.
> But God hath promised strength for the day,
> Rest for the labour, light for the way,
> Grace for the trials, help from above,
> Unfailing sympathy, undying love.
>
> ANNIE JOHNSON FLINT

Actually there is always something for which to be thankful, and this is illustrated by an incident that is said to have taken place during a worship service in one of the mountain churches in western North Carolina. During a part of the service in which each one was given an opportunity to relate his experiences in the Lord, one woman got up and said, "All I can say is, the Lord has nigh about ruined me!" And then she began to relate, one by one, the reverses in life that had come to her, and the various forms of adversity which she had encountered during the past year. When she was through speaking and had sat down, another elderly woman who had likewise suffered many reverses in life, and who was apparently stung by the sour note of bitterness echoed by the one who had just spoken, arose and said, "Well, all I can say is that I haven't got but two teeth left in my mouth, but thank the Lord they both meet!"

Dr. B. B. McKinney, widely known musician and song writer, once told of his mother who was widowed by the death of his father when he was very small. Left with a number of children and without adequate financial means with which to care for them, she had to work very hard and often late into the night. He told how his mother would often sing as she worked, and that at times, as he grew older, he wondered how she had been able to sing as she did under the heavy work load that she carried and in the face of so many unfavorable turns of circumstance. Then he added, "There is one song she sang more often than all other songs, and as I analyzed the meaning of the song, and understood its message, I not only knew how my mother was able to sing as she did, but also how she was able to keep her head up and face the world."

Later, Dr. McKinney set the words of "Never Alone" to music as he remembered her singing them:

> I've seen the lightning flashing,
> And heard the thunder roll,
> I've felt sin's breakers dashing,
> Trying to conquer my soul;
> I've heard the voice of Jesus,
> Telling me still to fight on,
> He promised never to leave me,
> Never to leave me alone.
>
> —ANONYMOUS

Even so, the children of God can rejoice in spite of all the overwhelming deluges of circumstance; for heavenly joy springs from the God-man relationship and is rooted and grounded in faith—faith in him who is able to do far more than we ask or think.

EXERCISE

Take a clean white sheet of paper and a pencil, open your Bible at Philippians 4:4-9, find a quiet place where you will be completely alone (and without interruption), and sit down for a season of meditation.

Read the above passage of Scripture very carefully and then go back to verse 4 which says, "Rejoice in the Lord at all times; again I will say rejoice continually."

Then close your eyes and slowly repeat the words of verse 4, again and again. After you have done so, take the sheet of paper and write at the top of the page these words: "Bless-

Step 1

ings That Have Come to Me Over the Years"—then list the blessings one by one. Commence with your childhood, and then, in the intervening years, try to set down every type of blessing you have experienced in which there was cause for rejoicing.

Think of the home in which you were born. Think of your parents. If you are married, think of your wife or husband—and your children (if you are a parent). Think of your friends, your neighbors. Think of the lovely music that appeals to you . . . the songs you love to sing.

Think of the books you have read and of special passages that have brought joy to your heart. Think of places you have been and in which you found great delight.

Think of the seasons—the springtime with its much-varied hues of green; the summer with the fields of growing crops approaching harvest; the autumn and the kaleidoscopic beauty of the colors throughout the countryside; the winter with the freshly fallen snows—the sleet and the rain!

Then think of the Christian experiences that you have had—if you have been fortunate enough to have such.

Think of the Bible and the moments of fellowship you have had with God in prayer!

Think of the church and the beauty of her role as the matrix from which the good and perfect gifts from above find noblest expression.

Then close your eyes again and say, in spirit and in truth, "With God's help, I will rejoice in the Lord at all times; again I will say rejoice continually."

Step 2
Manifest Sweet Reasonableness

Your forbearance is to be known to all men (Phil. 4:5a).

   In the delta of ancient Egypt there was cultivated a tall water plant of the sedge family that came to be called the paper reed *(cyperus papyrus)*. The plant was used for a variety of purposes, but more especially as a source of writing material. Even today the plant may be found in the upper Nile regions and in Abyssinia, though it is extinct in lower Egypt. According to the description given by Theophrastus, the plant grew in shallow water with a root the thickness of a man's wrist. The root lay horizontally and sometimes would extend as much as fifteen feet in length. Small roots from the principal root would push down into the mud, and the main stem of the plant would grow to a height of as much as six feet. Pliny tells us that the cellular pith within the rind of the stem was cut into longitudinal strips which were laid side by side until the required width was gained, and then there was laid crosswise another layer of shorter strips at right angles. The two layers of the pith were thus "woven" together by a process which resulted in the formation of a sheet that was then soaked in the water of the Nile. By some means, whether by a paste as Pliny suggests or by means of glutinous matter contained in the material itself, the sheet was finally hammered into being and then dried in the sun. The rough places were leveled by polishing with a smooth shell or with ivory.

On such sheets of writing material, some of the earliest recorded messages, written in the years that antedate the Christian century, have come down to us. Many of the writings were lost to human eye beneath the drifting sands of the desert of the Middle East where rain seldom falls.

On one of these ancient fragments of papyrus the Greek word *epieikes* (translated "moderation" in Paul's letter to the Philippians) is used to mean "goodness and reasonableness." In another papyri fragment the word is used of a man who had been elected to public office and was said to have discharged his duties "in an equitable manner." In another fragment the word is used for the idea *right:* "The senators said, 'The Prytanis has done right.'"[1]

The word *(epieikeia)* translated "moderation" is one of the most difficult of all Greek words to translate. This difficulty is reflected clearly in the various translations of it. Wycliffe, for instance, translated it *patience,* while Tyndale and Cranmer translated it *softness.* The Geneva Bible has *the patient mind* while the Revised Standard Version has *forbearance,* as does Moffatt, but Weymouth has *forbearing spirit*. C. Kingsley Williams has: Let all the world know that you will *meet a man halfway*.[2]

The ancient Greeks held that *epieikeia* (moderation) was "justice and something better than justice." In the words of William Barclay, "A man has the quality of *epieikeia* if he knows when *not* to apply the strict letter of the law, if he knows when to relax justice and to introduce mercy. . . . *Epieikeia* is the quality of the man who knows that rules and regulations are not the last word; it is the quality of the man who knows when not to apply the letter of the law."[3]

The Christian then is the person who goes beyond mere justice in his evaluation of a given situation. He thinks of the woman who was taken in adultery and brought before Jesus who would have had her stoned to death had he applied the

Step 2

letter of the law; instead, Jesus went beyond justice.

Joseph Hall, the bishop of Norwich (1574-1676), said in his introduction to *Christian Moderation* that "Moderation is the silken string running through the pearl chain of all virtues." Euripides called moderation "the noblest gift of heaven."

The ability to take a moderate stance in the face of disturbing crises stems, in part, from the disciplines of youth. If one as a child is given to temper tantrums and to noisy, irrational responses to difficult situations, then that same trait of character is apt to be manifest in later years by the individual.

It is not possible by nature or temperament for every individual to react in a crisis, or in the face of unpleasant circumstance, with the phlegmatic mood of the Indian. And few of us are able to assume the role of the Stoic by manifesting abject indifference whether to pleasure or to pain. Stoic philosophy, founded by Zeno around 300 BC, taught that a man should never be subdued by passion but rather should remain free from passion, whether in the midst of joy or of sorrow. He should always be willing to submit to the circumstances of natural law, however gravely he might be affected by such, in a calm, heroic manner.

One does not have to react as an emotionless being in the face of upsetting circumstances—such as the French would call cul-de-sac (literally, bottom of a bag). On the other hand, one should face the issue responsibly, for the mark of a true adult is reflected in the cool, objective manner in which the person involved first evaluates and then deals realistically with the problem at hand.

It is not given for one to achieve all of the desired objectives in life. There was a young athlete, for instance, who had surpassed others in his agility, strength, prowess, and skill as he participated in the intramural sports of high school. In truth he had become the celebrity of his classmates—all eyes were upon him. It was his picture, his plays, that received the headlines in the local paper.

Unfortunately the young athlete received a grave injury in a football game that barred him from further participation in athletics. To the amazement of his friends, as he was confronted with the necessity of pursuing a new life-style, he reacted to his discomfiture with perfect poise. He showed little frustration and developed nothing of the mood of one who has been completely overwhelmed! Rather, he quietly announced to his friends: "Now that I can no longer be an athlete, I have decided that I will try to qualify myself as a sports reporter. With my athletic experience, I should have some advantage in reporting the playing of others!"

Many of the confrontations in life that lead to serious life situations that are filled with regret take place because the individuals involved fail to pause and think matters over fully. When something unpleasant has happened, and especially where there has been personal offense, it is a good idea to let some time pass before any responsive action. If one sleeps on the matter for a night, he is apt to have a clearer perspective in the morning. It is somewhat like climbing a high mountain and taking a fresh view of the land about you. You see the spread of the land in an altogether different way when you see it from a higher point of observation. Even so, allowing a bit of time to pass following a personal injury or an unpleasant encounter makes for a better view.

After all, the matter of greatest importance should not be what your enemies or friends immediately think of you with reference to a given matter; rather, it is what they will think of you when you and they are farther removed from the piquant or abrasive situation. The manner in which persons react to the trying moments of life reflect their true stature—how disciplined they are, how well in control of themselves.

There was an old saying in the mountains where I grew up,

Step 2

"You better watch the fellow who, in the face of a trying moment, does not fly into a rage, foam at the mouth, and tear into you, but rather stands either looking you in the eye, or staring out into space as though he were completely detached." That kind of a fellow is making up his mind and trying to decide what the wise course of action is for him to take, and in the least expected moment, you may get from him the surprise of your life!

One should always remember that there are some life situations that are merely a part of the passing scenes of life, and are therefore to be met with quiet courage and the ability to forget. William Lloyd Garrison put it this way: "With reasonable men, I will reason; with humane men, I will plead; but to tyrants, I will give no quarter, nor waste arguments where they will certainly be lost."[4]

Words, gentle or harsh, in a sense are as arrows—they fly away. And though the arrow be retrieved, if it landed in the human heart, the mark left by the arrow will long remain. As the poet said:

> I shot an arrow into the air,
> It fell to earth, I knew not where;
> For, so swiftly it flew, the sight
> Could not follow it in its flight.
>
> I breathed a song into the air,
> It fell to earth, I knew not where;
> For who has sight so keen and strong,
> That it can follow the flight of song?
>
> Long, long afterward, in an oak
> I found the arrow, still unbroke;
> And the song, from beginning to end,
> I found again in the heart of a friend.[5]

The Scriptures have much to say about moderation, reasonableness, and resentment. In Proverbs 15:1, we read: "A soft answer turneth away wrath; But a grievous word stirreth up anger." And again in Proverbs 19:11: "The discretion of a man maketh him slow to anger; And it is his glory to pass over a transgression." To quote Edward Bulwer-Lytton, "Great men gain doubly when they make foes their friends."[6]

The writer of Ecclesiastes has a word that all might ponder: "Be not righteous overmuch; neither make thyself overwise: why shouldest thou destroy thyself?" (7:16). And Paul in his letter to the Corinthians said, "Every man that striveth in the games exerciseth self-control in all things" (1 Cor. 9:25). And again, "The fruit of the Spirit is . . . temperance" (Gal. 5:22-23, KJV).

The secret to moderation lies in the admonition of Jesus in Luke 6:31: "And as ye would that men should do to you, do ye also to them likewise." This is the Golden Rule—the primal law of moderation—doing unto others as you would have others to do unto you. This is the value standard that could literally transform the conduct of people everywhere.

This is the approach that I have personally found to be a wonderful safeguard in times of crisis where confrontation is involved. After taking time to think the matter over and the course of action that should be wisest and best, I like to defer to Jesus, saying to myself, "What would Jesus do? What would be his response in such a life situation? Would he react with anger? Would there be any disposition on his part to retaliate? And what would he have me do?"

Jesus is our Good Shepherd. He is the one who goes before us. He is our great high priest. Consider the words spoken of him by the writer of the Book of Hebrews (4:14-16): "Having then a great high priest, who hath passed through the heavens, Jesus the Son of God, let us hold fast our confession. For we have not a high priest that cannot be touched with the feeling of our infirmities; but one that hath been in all points tempted like as we are, yet without sin. Let us therefore draw near with boldness unto the throne of grace, that we may receive mercy, and may find grace to help us in time of need." Jesus did not dwell apart from man. He identified himself completely with people; and in his identity, he emerged sinless.

Jesus experienced the tensions of sin. He knew the depths of sin. He was bruised by the assaults of sin. For forty days in the wilderness he was confronted with the tempter. He knew temptation at its fiercest, but he was not vanquished. He was tempted in all points as we, and yet without sin. And herein lies the difference between Jesus and mankind. He did not yield to sin. But more than this is true of Jesus. There was no latent sin in him to be stirred by temptation—and no habits of sin to be overcome.

But Jesus did know the weaknesses that are common to mankind. He knew hunger. He knew thirst. He experienced weariness. And it was at this point that Satan employed his strongest weapons against him, repeatedly, but without success. Jesus remained "undefiled" in a world that was full of sin. He remained sinless!

Most of us fall to temptation long before the tempter has unleashed the supreme power of his might against us. As another has said, "We are easily vanquished; we never know temptation at its fiercest and at its most terrible, because we fall long before that stage is reached. But Jesus was tempted as we are—and far beyond what we are. For in His case the tempter put everything he possessed into the assault, and Jesus withstood it."[7]

Consider Jesus and pain. He endured pain. He experienced the agony of sufferings just as we. Yet he did so without sin.

We are told that the human frame can only endure pain up to a certain point, for every person has a pain threshold. The threshold varies according to the individual. After a given stage of pain is reached, a person may faint. He thereby enters into a temporary door of escape from the agony of the moment by losing consciousness. The very fact that he collapses under the strain of physical pain or mental trauma indicates that there are agonies of pain unknown to him.

Jesus had no pain threshold. He took the worst that the enemies of his mission could fling against him. He did not flinch. He did not complain. He did not cry out for human sympathy. He did not retaliate. In temptation, most men collapse before they enter the fiercest stage. But Jesus did not collapse at all. Stage after stage found him calm and steadfast. We can say that Jesus was tempted in all points as we, and yet without sin, but no one of us can ever say that he has been tempted in all points as Jesus!

As one reflects upon Jesus, a new mood of concern for others comes over him. A spirit of sweet reasonableness, a mood of which he has never dreamed, begins to manifest itself in his life as he thinks on Jesus. He begins to have a new concept of mercy and understanding because Jesus was a person of mercy and understanding, and this was a completely new concept for the ancient world. It was unthinkable to the pagans to look upon their gods as gods of mercy.

To the Stoics, God was beyond all elements of feeling. To the Epicureans, the gods dwelt in *intermundia,* the spaces between the worlds—in utter detachment. Such "gods" were completely unaware of the world as such. Plutarch held that it was nothing less than blasphemous "to involve God in the affairs of this world." One can see therefore how staggering the concept of a sympathetic God must have been to those faraway thinkers. The idea of the untouchable God somehow had to go! And it did go when Jesus came.

The very fact that Jesus was tempted in all points as we, and yet without sin, means that he knows our afflictions—our burdens, our frustrations, our sorrows, our cares. And when one knows, he begins to have mercy. As another has said, "To

Step 2

know all is to forgive all." And no word is more applicable to Jesus.

Jesus is able to say to mankind at every point of temptation, at every instance of personal injury, in the face of every insult and cynical denouncement: "I have been there, too. I know how you feel. I understand your problem." Jesus traveled all of the roads of frustration, of disappointment, of bewildering doubt that lie before us.

The physical suffering of Jesus, however, was not the great suffering of his life. Scores of people have likely died with as great physical suffering as Jesus experienced. On the battlefields they have thus died without number. The suffering of Jesus was different. His disappointments, his frustrations, his bewildering confrontations were unlike those ever suffered by human beings. He was the perfect man. He was the great lover of the whole world. He loved the rich. He loved the poor. He loved the weak, the strong. He loved the worst of sinners! And he had mercy for them all.

Jesus knows our life. He is able to sympathize with us in our trials. He is ready to grant us his mercy for our sins. And nothing short of his mercy, and the experience of his grace, can so change our hearts until moderation comes and sweet reasonableness; and by so much, a new world order!

Think of Jesus on the cross. There he was, dying at the hands of the bitterest enemies man ever knew. There he was, suffering the greatest of human indecencies—dying the type of death that no Roman citizen was required to die. And yet there was no anger, no caustic thoughts of recrimination, no retaliation. Only sweet reasonableness. His only thoughts for his enemies were thoughts of mercy. That is why he said, "Father, forgive them; for they know not what they do" (Luke 23:34).

But why should the follower of Jesus undertake to be this sort of person? Why should a person have to endeavor to manifest the gracious, gentle mood of Jesus in life?

> Because, says Paul, the Lord is at hand. If we remember the coming triumph of Christ, then we can never lose our hope and our joy. If we remember that life is short, and that the end comes, then we will not wish to enforce the stern justice which so often divides men; we will wish to deal with men in love, as we hope that God will deal with us. Justice is human, but *epieikeia [sweet reasonableness]* is divine.[8]

EXERCISE

Take your Bible, your pen, and a clean sheet of paper and go apart to a quiet place where you can be, for a season, alone with your thoughts and with the Savior.

Read Isaiah 53:7; Luke 23:34; 1 Peter 2:21-25; and Matthew 5:48. Then kneel and pray.

After this, list on the paper a few specific instances of unreasonableness in your own life and in the lives of others . . . experiences like that of the pastor who went to the office of a member to try to bring about reconciliation over a matter but who was turned down, heartlessly and flatly, with the words, "It's too late now!" and the deacons who, with the pastor, were trying to reconcile two brothers who were feuding with each other, when one of the estranged brothers said, angrily, "I'll never budge an inch"; and the pastor who went to an estranged member who had become personally offended by a recent sermon that touched on a major sin in the member's life—a sin of which the pastor was unaware—and who stubbornly refused to be reconciled with the pastor who fell at his feet, kneeling, and "praying with much weeping." Then meditate on them, in the light of the above readings and ask yourself these questions: "What would have been the response of Jesus to each of these life situations had he been in my place or in theirs? What would Jesus have me do?"

Then kneel and pray . . . and listen for God's voice!

Step 3
Be Conscious of the Lord's Presence

The Lord is near (Phil. 4:5b).

If it seems unreasonable to hope for the followers of Jesus to experience, in any great measure, the two qualities of Christian character I have just discussed—the qualities of joy and sweet reasonableness—let us think of the basis and the reason for these qualities.

Both the basis and the reason for one's ability to achieve these qualities lie in the believer's consciousness of the Lord's presence. That is why Paul added, at the close of his admonition to strive for such, "The Lord is near" (Phil. 4:5).

The word translated *near* which Paul used here is an adverb and has the general idea of "place," as of something "near," or "close at hand." But the element of time is also present in some of the usages as of something "nigh, at hand." It is used of something drawing near as of one "nearly blind." The adverb is also used to express the idea of one near to the point of death.

The expression *near,* or *at hand* as appears in the Revised Standard Version, can have a double meaning. "The Spirit of the Lord is *here* with us, as we seek to do his will; but" the Lord himself is "to come again in final triumph as Jesus promised when he took leave of his disciples on the Mount of Olives at the time of the ascension. The believer has the triumph of his presence, in the Spirit, now, while in the flesh; but the coming triumph of Christ is to be at the last day, when we shall see him as he is, and when he will be in our midst forever to give us light."[1]

The idea of Christ's return is a strange doctrine to many contemporary minds. Such thoughts are foreign to the ways of those who live only in the present and think of the future in the terms of the materialist, who sees nothing beyond death but decay!

The whole premise of the apostle Paul, as he discussed the matter of peace in the human heart, rests upon the assumption that the individual is one who has already come to know Jesus as Savior and Lord. In knowing him he accepts his words of promise not because he can prove them (as the scientist would in dealing with physical properties in the laboratory) but rather because of his faith, faith that is genuine and a continuing part of his existence. Such a person has had a viable spiritual experience (such as Jesus discussed with Nicodemus—John 3:1-15) that has brought him into a vital relationship with the redeeming love of God and his boundless concern for mankind. He no longer doubts God's Word, but accepts it as the basis of all existence. Like the apostle Paul, he stands "persuaded" and nothing can move him from that position of hope.

This unwavering faith in the ultimate triumph of Christ, and of Christ's hope for the redeemed, is the real source of a Christian's moderation in his relationship with others. He has come to know, with the ancient Greeks in their use of the word *epieikeia* which Paul used here for "moderation" and which we translate "sweet reasonableness," that there is "justice and something better than justice." The ancient Greeks knew that there have to be laws in an orderly society; there have to be regulations governing the conduct of persons who live together in that society. But they also knew that there are times when a law, however just in theory, might become unjust in application. Even so the Christian, because of his eternal hope in Christ and the unshakable conviction of his own triumph in the end, becomes able "to relax justice and to introduce mercy."[2]

This quality of sweet reasonableness enables one to see beyond the mere letter of the law just as Jesus did in the case of the woman taken in adultery. Had Jesus followed the letter of the law, he would have sentenced the woman to be stoned, and that would have been a true application of justice to her according to the ancient laws of Israel. But Jesus went beyond the law and applied mercy in the hope of total redemption for the sinful woman.

Who of us today, by the sheer law of justice, would merit anything but God's condemnation? We know, as Paul said so well, that it is not "by works done in righteousness, which we did ourselves, but according to his mercy he saved us" (Titus 3:5).

This abiding faith in the Lord's presence becomes as an anchor for all our hopes and as a springboard for a just and righteous response to every human situation. The true child of God, the kingdom person, knows there is more to life than mere justice in human interpersonal relationships with his fellowmen. After all, does not God's Word say, "Render to no man evil for evil. Take thought for things honorable in the sight of all men. If it be possible, as much as in you lieth, be at peace with all men. Avenge not yourselves, beloved, but give place unto the wrath of God: for it is written, Vengeance belongeth unto me; I will recompense, saith the Lord. But if thine enemy hunger, feed him; if he thirst, give him to drink: for in so doing thou shalt heap coals of fire upon his head" (Rom. 12:17-21).

What is more, did not Jesus himself say, "Love your enemies, and pray for them that persecute you" (Matt. 5:44)?

"Foolish words," one may say who does not know the Savior,

and who does not follow in his train, but if one truly knows Jesus and loves him and endeavors to serve him as Savior and Lord, he has no alternative. For did not the same Jesus say, "Ye are my friends, if ye do the things which I command you"? Jesus' command is to manifest the qualities of sweet reasonableness *(epieikeia)* in the face of every human situation; for, all the while, the follower of Jesus knows that he is "stretching myself forward to the things which are before" (Phil. 3:13*b*) as Paul put it, and is equally conscious that when his earthly house of this tabernacle comes to be "dissolved" he will have "a house not made with hands, eternal, in the heavens" (2 Cor. 5:1).

All of this concept of faith, this hope in the future, rests solidly upon the ultimate triumph of Christ—his promised return, for did he not say, "Let not your heart be troubled: believe in God, believe also in me. In my Father's house are many mansions; if it were not so, I would have told you; for I go to prepare a place for you. And if I go and prepare a place for you, I come again, and will receive you unto myself; that where I am, there ye may be also. And whither I go, ye know the way" (John 14:1-4)?

The presence of Jesus is not to be thought of merely as some far-off event, some objective realization in an uncharted future. He has promised to be with us now, this very moment, if we open our hearts to him. "I tell you the truth," said he, "it is expedient for you that I go away; for if I go not away, the Comforter will not come unto you; but if I go, I will send him unto you. And he, when he is come, will convict the world in respect of sin, and of righteousness, and of judgment" (John 16:7-8). And to his inner circle, as he gave the great commission to disciple all the nations, he concluded by saying, "And lo, I am with you always, even unto the end of the world" (Matt. 28:20).

Once in making my rounds among the sick, I visited an

elderly woman who was not far removed from the gate of death. Because she loved the out-of-doors so much—the fresh air, the singing of the birds in the nearby trees, and the beauty of the profusion of flowers that bloomed in the yard—the family had, at her request, brought her out into a shaded portion of the yard on a cot and left her there for a time in the late hours of the afternoon. I sat by her side as she lay there on the cot looking up into the quiet blue of the heavens. She began to talk of life and death and of the wonder and beauty of the pilgrimage that had been hers since she first came to know the Savior. Then quietly she said, "The journey has been so wonderful because he has always been with me; he has never put more upon my back in the way of this world's troubles than I could bear; yes, he has always been with me . . . and he is with me now!" And this is essentially what the apostle Paul was saying: "Always be conscious of the Lord's presence, for he is very near."

EXERCISE

Go to your quiet place of prayer, sit down, and close your eyes for a period of meditation. Turn then in your Bible and read Paul's words again—his words saying, "Rejoice in the Lord at all times. . . . Your forbearance is to be known to all men. The Lord is near" (Phil. 4:4-5).

Close your eyes again and contemplate Paul's words saying, again and again, "The Lord is at hand. . . . The Lord is near. . . . The Lord is nearby. . . . And I can feel his presence now!"

When you have done this, take your worksheet and write down, one after another, the experiences in your life which recall your earliest personal awareness of the presence of God. Think of your conversion experience—if you have come to know Jesus as Savior. Think of the great moments in your life when decisions were made on the basis of what you believed to be the divine will. Think of the various times when you had a special awareness of his presence.

When you have done this, think on the experiences of the great heroes of faith in the Bible who walked and talked with God and who had, in their own quiet moments like Jacob, their heavenly dream and saw in their own way angels both ascending and descending on heaven's ladder (Gen. 28:12).

Then pray this prayer (or one of your own wording) as you kneel with closed eyes: "Dear Heavenly Father, teach me how to rely, completely, upon thy divine promises. Make me, above all things, conscious of thy living presence—not only in my seasons of stress and whelming life situations, but also in the quiet times of life when I walk, and stand, and sit by untroubled waters. For this is my prayer, in Jesus' name. Amen."

Step 4
Avoid Overanxiety

Don't have the worrying habit (Phil. 4:6a).

In the foothills of the Blue Ridge Mountains of western North Carolina where I spent my childhood days, I would hear occasionally the expression, "Oh, he's a worrywart," or "Don't be a worrywart!" Such words were applied to the person who was given to overanxiety about little things.

Jesus must have had this type of person in mind when he said,

> Therefore I say unto you, Be not anxious for your life, what ye shall eat, or what ye shall drink; nor yet for your body, what ye shall put on. Is not the life more than the food, and the body than the raiment? Behold the birds of the heaven, that they sow not, neither do they reap, nor gather into barns; and your heavenly Father feedeth them. Are not ye of much more value than they? And which of you by being anxious can add one cubit unto the measure of his life? And why are ye anxious concerning raiment? Consider the lilies of the field, how they grow; they toil not, neither do they spin: yet I say unto you, that even Solomon in all his glory was not arrayed like one of these. But if God doth so clothe the grass of the field, which to-day is, and to-morrow is cast into the oven, shall he not much more clothe you, O ye of little faith? Be not therefore anxious, saying, What shall we eat? or, What shall we drink? or, Wherewithal shall we be clothed? For after all these things do the Gentiles seek; for your heavenly Father knoweth that ye have need of all these things. But seek ye first his kingdom, and his righteousness; and all these things shall be added unto you. Be not therefore anxious for the morrow: for the morrow will be anxious for itself. Sufficient unto the day is the evil thereof (Matt. 6:25-34).

Certainly there can be little peace of mind for the person who is given to overanxiety about material things. The apostle Paul evidently realized this, for he said in his letter to the Philippians, "Don't have the worrying habit" (Phil. 4:6a). The Revised Standard Version has, "Have no anxiety about anything." W. J. Conybeare has, "Let no care trouble you"; Montgomery has "Do not worry about anything"; and the Berkeley Version of the New Testament has, "Entertain no worry."

The Greek word *merimnate* in the passage which is translated "Have no anxiety" is a present imperative expressing prohibition. It comes from another ancient word *merimna* which in turn comes from the Greek word *merizo, merizomai,* which basically means "to be drawn in different directions," a meaning which we express in English by the word *distraction,* "distraction of mind."

The idea of "overanxiety" which Paul seems to have in mind in his word to the Philippians is apparently found in Matthew 6:25, and one finds the same idea in an ancient papyrus writing: "I am now writing in haste to prevent your being anxious, for I will see that you are not worried."[1]

In an old Phrygian inscription, one finds the proper name *Titedios Amerimnos*[2]; and at least one scholar, Ramsey, suggests that the name *Amerimnos* might have been a baptismal name given to Titedios at the time he became a Christian, setting him apart as one who is not "anxious for the morrow" (Matt. 6:34). Paul was merely saying here, "You are not to be overanxious about anything," and this amounts to saying, in substance, "Don't develop a dual (divided) personality over anything. Let the worst come; let the rivers of distress overflow all the banks of your concern, but do not let your mind become distracted."

A friend of mine told me about her behavior on the occasion of the destruction of her home by fire. When the fire broke out she was not more than a hundred yards away from the house, and she naturally rushed home as fast as she could.

The fire originated in the kitchen, and already that part of the house was enveloped in flames, but the flames had not yet reached the front part of the house, though there was some smoke in the hallway.

On her arrival at the fire, Mrs. Perkins said, "I was so distracted that I was completely beside myself! Immediately I opened the front door and cautiously made my way into the hall, going past the living room on the left and a bedroom on the right. I had ample time to have rescued a few of my most prized possessions, but my mind simply did not work that way; rather, my eyes fell upon an old bowl and pitcher on a washstand at the far end of the hall, nearest the fire, and I grabbed it up and rushed out of the house and just stood there in a state of complete bewilderment and watched the house burn to the ground!"

Another person, a housewife, told me of her reaction when a fire consumed a nearby tenant's house on their farm. She said, "I actually ran in circles around the house . . . almost like a chicken with its head cut off! I had plenty of time to enter the house and bring out a few of the things, but I was so excited and in such a state of confusion that I finally just stood still and watched as the flames invaded every room and finally enveloped the whole building."

It is quite natural for one to worry at times, and Paul is not saying that one is never to worry; he is rather telling us that we should not become *overanxious* and engage in *overworrying* at any time about anything.

Of course a mother with a gravely sick child is going to have great anxiety until the danger is passed. But the Christian is to maintain the poise of a faithful believer, always realizing, above and beyond the present, that God is in his heaven and looking down with his loving concern upon his children in their crises of life.

A verse in the Bible that has always meant much to me is found in Romans 8:28. The passage, as I had always read it in the King James Version, while comforting me, also bothered me greatly: "And we know that all things work together for good to them that love God, to them who are the called according to his purpose." I was never able to see how "all things" could "work together for good" even though one loves God and is "called" according to his purpose. That idea just did not satisfy me. Then I read one day that in one of the old manuscripts of the original text of the New Testament there is found in the margin the word *ho Theos,* meaning "the God." This suggested that perhaps in the original manuscript the word *God* was the subject of the verb *works.* Now one finds in the Revised Standard Version this translation: "We know that in everything God works for good with those who love him, who are called according to his purpose." Here we are told it is God who does the working for good, and he not only "works for good," but works together "with those who love him." The Christian therefore has "a partner" who not only works *with him,* but who works *for him* in the critical moments of life when waters of disappointment swirl about him.

In Christ, the believer can say, "Let the worst come. Let Satan do his utmost to overcome me. Still I will not be overwhelmed, for my Heavenly Father works with me and for me. He will help me to make the best out of the worst that comes my way!" And this is exactly how it works for those who have learned to lean upon God in perfect confidence and in perfect trust for salvation and wisdom and guidance in all of life's ways.

There are so many of us who seem merely to believe intellectually in Jesus. So many have not learned to lean upon him with their whole personality in absolute trust.

In Carrollton, Kentucky, I had an experience that I will always remember. Mr. T. M. Minish, the funeral director, invited me to go with him to a home out into the countryside where he was to place for the final viewing the body of an aged man who had just expired. The family was fearful of the ability of the elderly companion to stand up under the shocking impact of her husband's death, and Mr. Minish asked me to go along and speak words of comfort.

As the casket bearing the body was being tenderly placed in the living room of the home, and opened, I joined the elderly mother and other members of the family in the bedroom for words of consolation and prayer. Immediately the aged mother insisted that we must all go into the "parlor" where her loved one lay in death. The daughter felt that at the moment it might not be best for her mother to go in and look upon the cold face of her dead companion, but the mother insisted, and we went in together. I could never forget the grace and poise the old mother reflected as she stood in front of the casket, resting her warm hands upon the cold, folded hands of her lover. For a moment she was completely silent, and then, slowly, she began to speak and this is what she said: "For sixty years we walked together, side by side. He was my lover, and I was his love, and now he is gone and I shall have to walk alone." And then lifting her right hand and pointing upward with the index finger she said, "If it were not for him, I could not go on, but he is helping me. . . . He's helping me now!"

God is always at our side to encourage and strengthen us in our moments of trial when we look to him by faith, for faith is the substance of hope, and hope is the foundation of all understanding. And Paul said that those of us who profess to be followers of the Christ are not to be distracted, overanxious, about anything—and that means everything!

Death, of course, has often been regarded as "The Great Distractor." Even the thoughts of impending death can so gnaw at the soul of a person until the mind is all but torn apart.

Well do I recall an experience when a saintly woman, knowing that she was at the threshold of death, called for her pastor.

As I entered the room where the sick one lay, the aged mother turned to her children and said, "Would you all please allow the pastor and me to have a few moments together; I want to talk to him—alone."

As the family, one by one, left the room and closed the door, I drew my chair near to the side of the bed and leaned forward in waiting for her first word. After what seemed to be an age of silence, the mother, who was yet perfectly coordinate in her reasoning and speech, burst into tears, saying, "I don't want to die! I don't, I don't . . . I don't want to die!"

The very thought of death was distracting to her mind and overwhelming.

As best I could, I endeavored to help the mother "shift gears" (as I sometimes call it) with her mind, and began to talk to her about the glories of heaven and the wondrous beauty of our continuing relationship with the Savior. I recalled for her the words of Jesus to Martha at the grave of her brother Lazarus, saying, "Thy brother shall rise again. . . . I am the resurrection, and the life: he that believeth on me, though he die, yet shall he live; and whosoever liveth and believeth on me shall never die" (John 11:23 *ff.*). Then I called to her mind the words of Jesus in John 14, where he said, "Let not your heart be troubled: believe in God, believe also in me. In my father's house are many mansions; if it were not so, I would have told you; for I go to prepare a place for you. And if I go and prepare a place for you, I come again, and will receive you unto myself; that where I am, there ye may be also" (vv. 1-4).

Presently a quiet calm came over the dear soul as she centered her thoughts on Jesus and the hope of resurrection and his eternal, loving care. Actually it seemed that her fears left her completely for the moment, and why not, for did not

Step 4

John say, "There is no fear in love: but perfect love casteth out fear" (1 John 4:18)?

One of the great examples of Christian understanding, poise, and gracious response to the hour of death took place during my seminary days on the occasion of the death of the great Dr. A. T. Robertson, professor of Greek at The Southern Baptist Theological Seminary.

Dr. Robertson had met the class in senior Greek at 3:00 on the afternoon of Monday, the beginning of the second week of the 1933-1934 seminary year. He taught until 3:30, and then announced that he was adjourning the class because of the oppressive heat. Those of us in the class who knew him well were aware that something dreadful was happening. Already his face was tinged with cyanosis, and he was constantly mopping the massive beads of sweat from his forehead.

At 6:00 Dr. Robertson was dead.

Later in the evening I was asked to be one of the honor guards in the first watch of the night, and I arrived at the home around 9:00 PM.

From the hour of his death, Mrs. Robertson had remained in seclusion in the room just off the living room, but late in the evening she emerged and began to speak quietly with those of us who were to keep watch in the upper room by the couch upon which her loved one lay.

The scene of her standing there, with her hands behind her, and leaning against the facing of the door that led into the dining room is one that I will long recall. Her cheeks bore the mark of tears, but no tears were in evidence then. She stood with all the graceful majesty of a queen as she faced us and talked about her beloved husband. She recalled how only a few days before he had discussed with her the Scripture passage that tells of Jesus raising the little girl from death (Mark 5:41). She even quoted the very words of his own translation of the passage and spoke of his profound faith in the ability of God to raise the dead. She then went on and on and on in her gentle conversation about her husband and about immortality.

After reminding us that tea and coffee and cookies had been provided for us, she graciously expressed her deep appreciation for our presence, gave us her good wishes for the night, and left.

Somehow as I left the bedroom chamber where Dr. Robertson lay in death, past the midnight hour, I felt I had a deeper understanding of the meaning of death, of immortality, and of the comforting promise of Jesus concerning the afterlife. I also felt that for me, the thought of death and the grave had lost much of its sting and its victory, but more than this, I felt that henceforth I would endeavor to face all the vexations and disabling situations of life with greater Christian composure and understanding.

Well might the apostle Paul say, "You are not to be overanxious about anything"; and with the hymn writer we know that "Faith is the victory . . . that overcomes the world."

EXERCISE

Return to your quiet place and sit down for a season of meditation. Think on Paul's words of admonition. Think of the trying situations of life that you have witnessed where those involved seemed to be completely overwhelmed and filled with despair. Do you think they were really aware of the promises of Jesus and that they had come to trust in them fully? What was their relationship to the church? What was the measure of their day-to-day witness to their faith in Jesus?

Now think of individuals whom you have observed in similar crises but who reacted in an altogether different manner— individuals who, like Mrs. A. T. Robertson, were able to meet death face-to-face without flinching—even when confronted with the personal impact of its shocking power with such little warning. Then ponder their reaction, their calm, their poise, their strength. Endeavor to account for it in the light of their lives—if you knew them well. Think of what your own reaction might have been.

Turn now to Paul's words in Philippians 4:4-6 and read them again and again, until they are deeply fixed in your mind. Read also the following passages and meditate on each one after reading it: Psalm 31:9; 2 Samuel 22:7; Psalm 34:6; 2 Corinthians 1:3-4; 2 Corinthians 12:10; Psalm 46; Psalm 40:1-3; John 14:1-6; 2 Corinthians 4:17.

Then kneel and pray, as the Spirit gives you utterance, and ask God to help you lean upon him completely in every trying hour, in all the days to come—always believing, always trusting, always waiting patiently for his peace—knowing that "therein is revealed a righteousness of God from faith unto faith: as it is written, But the righteous shall live by faith" (Rom. 1:17).

Step 5
Be Prayerful

But in everything by prayer and entreaty with thanksgiving your requests are to be made known unto God (Phil. 4:6b).

In discussing with his Philippian friends the road to God's peace, had the apostle Paul concluded his admonition with the words, "Don't have the worrying habit," he would have left them wondering how such could ever be achieved. How can one, for instance, avoid overanxiety about the grave issues of life that, sooner or later, everyone is bound to face? How can one stop being anxious about a loved one who is wavering between life and death in spite of all that mortal hands can do? Consequently, Paul went on to say, "But in everything by prayer and entreaty with thanksgiving your requests are to be made known unto God."

The history of men of faith discloses that they were always men of prayer. Luther Rice, we are told, had many stated times in which he prayed daily. He prayed early in the morning. He prayed as the day wore on. He prayed in the afternoon. He prayed with and for the families where he spent his nights as an itinerant wayfarer, traveling up and down the Atlantic Coast in his effort to raise money for missions. He closed his day with prayer!

But Jesus is our great example in prayer, and in even a brief review of his life as recorded in the New Testament we find that prayer was as common to his life-style as the air he breathed.

Jesus opened the day with prayer, for we read that "In the morning, a great while before day, he rose up and went out, and departed into a desert place, and there prayed" (Mark 1:35).

He prayed at eventide: "After he had taken leave of them, he departed into the mountain to pray. And when even was come, the boat was in the midst of the sea, and he alone on the land" (Mark 6:46-47).

He began his life's work with prayer: "When all the people were baptized, . . . Jesus also having been baptized, and praying, the heaven was opened" (Luke 3:21).

Jesus prayed all night on at least one occasion, as Luke tells us: "And it came to pass in these days, that he went out into the mountain to pray; and he continued all night in prayer to God" (Luke 6:12).

He prayed with his friends: "And it came to pass about eight days after these sayings, that he took with him Peter and John and James, and went up into the mountain to pray" (Luke 9:28).

Jesus prayed in public: "At that season Jesus answered and said, I thank thee, O Father, Lord of heaven and earth, that thou didst hide these things from the wise and understanding" (Matt. 11:25; cf. John 17:1 *ff.*).

Jesus prayed in times of great crises, as in Gethsemane: "Then cometh Jesus with them unto a place called Gethsemane, and saith unto his disciples, Sit ye here, while I go yonder and pray" (Matt. 26:36).

He prayed for his followers saying, "Simon, Simon, behold, Satan asked to have you, that he might sift you as wheat: but I made supplication for thee, that thy faith fail not" (Luke 22:31-32).

Jesus called attention to power in prayer: "Thinkest thou that I cannot beseech my Father, and he shall even now send me more than twelve legions of angels?" (Matt. 26:53).

Step 5

At times Jesus knelt down to pray: "He was parted from them about a stone's cast; and he kneeled down and prayed" (Luke 22:41). And Matthew tells us that in the Gethsemane experience Jesus "went forward a little, and fell on his face, and prayed" (Matt. 26:39). Apparently Jesus prayed while standing and walking along with his disciples en route to Gethsemane, for John tells us that "lifting up his eyes to heaven, he said, Father, the hour is come; glorify thy Son, that the Son may glorify thee" (John 17:1).

Jesus instructed his disciples in prayer, saying, "In praying use not vain repetitions, as the Gentiles do: for they think that they shall be heard for their much speaking" (Matt. 6:7).

And again: "When ye pray, ye shall not be as the hypocrites: for they love to stand and pray in the synagogues and in the corners of the streets,that they may be seen of men. . . . But thou, when thou prayest, enter into thine inner chamber, and having shut thy door, pray to thy Father who is in secret, and thy Father who seeth in secret shall recompense thee" (Matt. 6:5-6).

Jesus did not mean to infer that one has to go into a regular prayer place, or special room, to pray. One may have an inner chamber anywhere. It can be on the street, as one walks along in the midst of busy traffic. It can be in an automobile, or an airplane, as one goes from place to place. It can be, for the business people, in their office, as they sit or kneel by their desk. The idea is to come into God's presence "alone."

Dr. W. Hersey Davis, in his expository lecture to his students on prayer, as "duty to God, or that which relates to God" (Matt. 6:5-15), discussed the manner in which the Pharisees approached God in prayer. They were, he said, "play-actors" courting applause. "They would indulge in ostentatious prayers at every chance. Christ says that you may get from prayer exactly what you seek. If you desire to be seen by men, you are paid in full; for you were seen—'sign the receipt!' And a multitude of words with fine rhetoric gains nothing. Rehearsed prayers in the pulpit or pew have little effect—yea, men praise them. The heathen have prayer wheels turned by the wind. And the formalist 'gets off' high-sounding periods. . . . And to think that God can be reached by repetitions is due to a degraded idea of how to reach and influence God. . . . And when we are in his presence, we are not to give him mere information, for he has that."[1] Dr. W. O. Carver used to say, "'There is no danger more subtle than to win a reputation for fluency, eloquence, power in prayer.'"[2]

Knowing how deeply his disciples needed instruction in the matter of prayer, Jesus gave to them the Model Prayer which we commonly refer to as "The Lord's Prayer." "After this manner therefore pray," he said: "Our Father who art in heaven, Hallowed be thy name. Thy kingdom come. Thy will be done, as in heaven, so on earth. Give us this day our daily bread. And forgive us our debts, As we also have forgiven our debtors. And bring us not into temptation, but deliver us from the evil one" (Matt. 6:9-13).

The idea of the Fatherhood of God was not yet developed among the Hebrews, as Christ revealed it. He sought to reveal God as a loving Father who can be approached by all—just as one may approach his human father.

> I am not the only one to whom he is Father. His sole interest is not in me. "I am praying to a Father who is equally the Father of all others who come to him" (Carver). *Hallowed be thy name*—let thy name be held holy. The first request is that God may be recognized in all the world as the holy God. *Thy kingdom come*—the reign of God in this world is to be our supreme concern. *Thy will be done*—the full reign of God means the supreme dominance of the will of God. *As in heaven* is the standard to which *on earth* is to attain. For our immediate necessities—not any and everything we may desire—we are to pray. Give us this day our daily bread—just provide physical support for the day that is ahead of us (whether the day ahead of us in the morning or at night). We have pressing spiritual needs. *Forgive us our debts, as we also have forgiven our debtors. Debts,* here mean sins. We cannot

> do our part in bringing God's kingdom in, in making his will supreme on earth, if we have the unforgiving spirit in the least. And when we ask his forgiveness, we are to have already forgiven our debtors. God forgives only the forgiving, is the meaning of verses 14 and 15. *Lead us not into temptation, but deliver us from the evil one.* Temptation is not sin, but yielding to temptation is sin. We are to be led by God, and we are to pray that God's leading may not bring us into temptation, for it is always a perilous ordeal. But if he leads, we must face it and in reliance on his grace come through it. And when the evil one besets us, we cannot rely upon our own strength; but following God's leading we shall be rescued from the power of the evil one.[3]

Life for the Philippians was anything but rosy. There was little about it that was bright and promising. The city of Philippi was located in ancient Macedonia near the river Gangites on a steep hill that overlooked an extensive coastal plain beside the highway that ran between Thessalonica and Neapolis. Originally called Crenides (fountains), Philip II of Macedon fortified the city in order to command the neighboring gold mines that lay nearby. Here in 42 BC, following the defeat of Brutus and Cassius by Octavius and Antony, Philippi became a Roman colony, a sort of buffer territory between Rome and the territory to the north. Paul visited the city twice and knew the people and their surroundings well. Once a prosperous city—in the heyday of its gold mines—the city was now without prosperity, and its people were poor. The prime days of vigor, health, beauty, and prosperity were gone!

In speaking of the offering of the Macedonians in behalf of the poor in Jerusalem, Paul told how the grace of God was shown in the churches of Macedonia: "That in much proof of affliction the abundance of their joy and their deep poverty abounded unto the riches of their liberality. For according to their power, I bear witness," he said, "yea and beyond their power, they gave of their own accord" (2 Cor. 8:1-3). Paul also recounted how they entreated him to allow them to share in the offering: "Beseeching us with much entreaty in regard of this grace and the fellowship in the ministering to the saints"

(2 Cor. 8:4). Add to this the fact that for one even to be a follower of Jesus, then, was a dangerous, hazardous thing.

Listen to Paul as he tells of his own sufferings as a follower of Christ:

> Of the Jews five times received I forty stripes save one. Thrice was I beaten with rods, once was I stoned, thrice I suffered shipwreck, a night and a day have I been in the deep; in journeyings often, in perils of rivers, in perils of robbers, in perils from my countrymen, in perils from the Gentiles, in perils in the city, in perils in the wilderness, in perils in the sea, in perils among false brethern; in labor and travail, in watchings often, in hunger and thirst, in fastings often, in cold and nakedness (2 Cor. 11:24-27).

Even so, the writer of the Book of Hebrews tells how "others had trial of mockings and scourgings, yea, moreover of bonds and imprisonment: they were stoned, they were sawn asunder, they were tempted, they were slain with the sword: they went about in sheepskins, in goatskins; being destitute, afflicted, ill-treated (of whom the world was not worthy), wandering in deserts and mountains and caves, and the holes of the earth" (Heb. 11:36-38).

In the face of all of this, said Paul, the way not to worry and to have peace is to pray. Paul told us that we are to take everything to God in prayer; and in everything by prayer and supplication with thanksgiving we are to let our requests be made known to God. "Peace," said M. R. Vincent, "is the fruit of believing prayer."

> More things are wrought by prayer
> Than this world dreams of. Wherefore,
>   let thy voice
> Rise like a fountain for me night and day.[4]

Jesus said, "Verily I say unto you, Except ye turn, and become as little children, ye shall in no wise enter into the

Step 5

kingdom of heaven" (Matt. 18:3). A little child does not hesitate in turning to its parents when anything unpleasant comes. The child knows that its father and mother are concerned about him and that no matter what happens they will be on his side. Nothing is more beautiful than to see a little child turn to its mother or father in the face of the little wounds, frustrations, and disappointments that bruise and hurt. As another has said, "He tells them all, never doubting that his parents will be ready and willing to listen to him. We should be exactly so with God."[5]

Even so, we should go to our Heavenly Father and make known to him all our requests: "We can pray for *ourselves*. We can pray for forgiveness for the *past,* for the things we need in the *present,* and for help and guidance for the *future*. We can take our own past and present and future, with all our shame, with all our needs, with all our fears, into the presence of God. We can pray for *others*. We can commend to God's care those near and far who are forever within our memories and within our hearts."[6]

Paul reminded us, however, that the spirit of thanksgiving is to accompany all our prayers and supplications as we make them known to him. Just as one is to go to the Heavenly Father in prayer about anything and everything that affects one's life, so one is to give thanks in *everything*. Whether in joy or in sorrow, one is always to realize that things can be worse than they are. The spirit of thanksgiving implies more than mere *gratitude;* it is an indication of one's "*perfect submission* to the will of God"[7] who helps us to make the best out of the worst that comes our way and always works with us and works for us—and that unto our good!

EXERCISE

Take your Bible and go to your quiet place, sit down, and read the following passages of Scripture:

"Jehovah . . . heareth the prayer of the righteous" (Prov. 15:29).

"Ye shall seek me, and find me, when ye shall search for me with all your heart" (Jer. 29:13).

"Ask, and it shall be given you; seek, and ye shall find; knock, and it shall be opened unto you" (Matt. 7:7).

"Seek ye Jehovah and his strength;
Seek his face evermore" (1 Chron. 16:11).

"In the shadow of thy wings will I take refuge" (Ps. 57:1).

"Blessed is the man that heareth me,
Watching daily at my gates,
Waiting at the posts of my doors" (Prov. 8:34).

"When ye pray, ye shall not be as the hypocrites: . . . that they may be seen of men" (Matt. 6:5-7).

Men "ought always to pray, and not to faint" (Luke 18:1).

"Jehovah hath given me my petition which I asked of him" (1 Sam. 1:27).

"In the time of their trouble, when they cried unto thee, thou heardest from heaven" (Neh. 9:27).

"If two of you shall agree on earth as touching anything that they shall ask, it shall be done for them of my Father who is in heaven" (Matt. 18:19).

"Therefore I say unto you, All things whatsoever ye pray and ask for, believe that ye receive them, and ye shall have them" (Mark 11:24).

"If any man be a worshipper of God, and do his will, him he heareth" (John 9:31).

"If ye abide in me, and my words abide in you, ask whatsoever ye will, and it shall be done unto you" (John 15:7).

"Ye ask, and receive not, because ye ask amiss, that ye may spend it in your pleasures" (Jas. 4:3).

"The supplication of a righteous man availeth much" (Jas. 5:16).

"Whatsoever we ask we receive of him, because we keep

Step 5

his commandments and do the things that are pleasing in his sight" (1 John 3:22).

One must always remember, however, that effective prayers must rest solidly upon the foundation of unshakable faith. And what is faith but the leaning of the total human personality upon God for salvation, for wisdom, for guidance, for strength, for peace? Even as James has said, "But let him ask in faith, nothing doubting: for he that doubteth is like the surge of the sea driven by the wind and tossed. For let not that man think that he shall receive anything of the Lord; a doubleminded man, unstable in all his ways" (Jas. 1:6-8).

Having read, thoughtfully, the above passages, kneel and engage in a season of prayer to the Heavenly Father, praying not merely for yourself but for others who may or may not be dear to you, and the Father will hear you.

Do not pray for easy tasks. Pray to be stronger! Pray with a confessing heart: "Confess therefore your sins one to another, and pray for one another, that ye may be healed" (Jas. 5:16).

"Wisdom is the principal thing; therefore get wisdom;
  Yea, with all thy getting get understanding" (Prov. 4:7).

Lastly, consider your own past prayer life. When did you last pray seriously? Recall, if you can, the substance of your last prayer. For what and for whom did you pray? Was your prayer self-centered? Did your prayer have in it the mood of the Model Prayer which Jesus taught us to pray? Then kneel again and await his voice and the impressions that follow, for you will be aware of his presence!

Step 6
Think Good Thoughts

Finally, brethren, whatever things are true, whatever things are worthy of respect, whatever things are righteous, whatever things are pure, whatever things are lovely, whatever things are of good report, if anything (is) *moral excellence and if anything* (is) *praise, keep on thinking about these things (Phil. 4:8-9a).*

There are probably many directions which our minds take at different times, and under different circumstances, but many minds tend to have a "set" or "groove" in which they operate. Paul knew this and that is why he was eager for the Philippians to set their minds on the things that are right. It is extremely important that one understand this principle, for "it is a law of life that, if a man thinks of something often enough and long enough, he will come to the stage when he cannot stop thinking about it."[1]

The ancient Greeks held that there are some things, for instance, that should not even be named, much less discussed; for to talk about a thing—to name it and let it become commonplace in the conversation—is to bring one a step nearer to its acceptance.

As a man thinks in his heart, so is he, for the roots of all deliberate action lie in the heart. If the heart is impure, the thoughts that spring from the heart will be impure. "Through wisdom is a house builded," said the wise man of old, "And by understanding it is established" (Prov. 24:3).

In calling his people back to a closer walk with God, the

prophet Isaiah said, "Let the wicked forsake his way, and the unrighteous man his thoughts; and let him return unto Jehovah, and he will have mercy upon him" (55:7). And Paul spoke in his letter to the Corinthians of how we cast down "imaginations, and every high thing that is exalted against the knowledge of God, and bringing every thought into captivity to the obedience of Christ" (2 Cor. 10:5).

All of us have a definite life-style in our thoughts. Some have a tendency to look on the bright side of life—to see the best and to hope for the best in all things. Others are of a gloomy disposition and tend to have a dispirited mind like the person who said, "The sun may be shining today, but you wait till tomorrow!"

One can become contaminated by his own thoughts and work himself into a groove or thought pattern from which he is unable to extricate himself.

Once I went to a home to minister where a person had committed suicide. The man, early in the morning, had loaded his rifle as though to go out for target shooting, but instead he walked down to the barn, and, when well out of view of the house, shot himself dead.

Later in the day, I began to inquire of family and friends as to the motivation for the suicide. There was one point at which all friends with whom I talked agreed: he was a man of a gloomy disposition and great loneliness. He sought the company of no one. One neighbor said, "He would often speak as though he did not have a friend on earth; in fact, he said as much recently when he was talking with me. He was always downcast in spirit. No one ever saw him smile. No one ever heard him speak hopefully about anything. He always wore the garments of gloom!"

In Jeremiah 29:11, we read, "For I know the thoughts that I think toward you, saith Jehovah, thoughts of peace, and not of evil, to give you hope in your latter end." This is why it is so important that one set his thoughts upon the things of God, for in thinking on the ways of God, the thoughts of God, and the plan of God for our lives, we come to have "a future and a hope." What is more, the Bible says, "Ye shall seek me, and find me, when ye shall search for me with all your heart. And I will be found of you, saith Jehovah, and I will turn again your captivity" (Jer. 29:13-14).

The apostle Paul, in establishing guideposts along the path to peace, introduced six adjectives which have to do with Christian ideals, "old-fashioned and familiar words not necessarily from any philosophic list of moral excellencies Stoic or otherwise. Without these no ideals can exist."[2]

It is interesting to note that Paul introduced this list of the fine things on which people are to set their thoughts with the word *finally*. What he meant is "from now on——that is, in the light of what he has just said concerning the other steps on the road to peace. This new life-style of thoughts is to prevail at all times, with regard to all matters.

First, the pilgrim is to set his mind on the things that are *true*. The word Paul used here for "true" is an old Greek word that has the meaning of *true* as over against *false*. Some of the things in this world are illusory and deceptive. "They promise that which they can never perform. They offer a man a specious peace and happiness which, in fact, they can never supply. A man should always set his thoughts on the things on which he can rely, the things which will not fail him, or let him down."[3] The psalmist said,

> I have chosen the way of faithfulness:
> Thine ordinances have I set before me.
> I cleave unto thy testimonies:
> O Jehovah, put me not to shame.
> I will run the way of thy commandments,
> When thou shalt enlarge my heart (Ps. 119:30-32).

The source of all truth, of course, is Jesus Christ: "For the law was given through Moses; grace and truth came through Jesus Christ" (John 1:17). This is true because he is "the image of the invisible God, the firstborn of all creation; for in him were all things created, in the heavens and upon the earth, things visible and things invisible, whether thrones or dominions or principalities or powers; all things have been created through him, and unto him; and he is before all things, and in him all things consist. And he is the head of the body, the church: who is the beginning, the firstborn from the dead; that in all things he might have the preëminence. For it was the good pleasure of the Father that in him should all the fulness dwell; and through him to reconcile all things unto himself, having made peace through the blood of his cross; through him, I say, whether things upon the earth, or things in the heavens" (Col. 1:15-20).

Truth is the fundamental footing, the ultimate in foundation for the setting of the pattern for one's thought. Paul spoke of truth as one of the cardinal elements in moral rearmament: "Therefore, take up the complete armor of God in order that you may be able to withstand in the evil day, and having accomplished all still to stand victoriously. Take your stand therefore having girded your loins with truth" (Eph. 6:13-14).

Second, the Christian is to set his mind on the things that are *honorable*—things that are marked by "the dignity of holiness." The King James Version has "whatsoever things are honest" in the sense of "honorable" as one finds in the Revised Standard Version. The word Paul used is the Greek word *semnos* which conveys the idea of "grave, worthy of respect." This is why the Revised Standard Version suggests in the margin of the translation *reverend*.

The word *semnos* is not an easy word to translate, for it is a word that was commonly used of the gods and of the temples of the pagan gods. When used with reference to a man, it portrays a person who, as another has said, "moves through-

Step 6

out the world as if the whole world were the temple of God." Matthew Arnold translates the word "nobly serious."

There is much in the world which is cheap, flippant, ephemeral, but Paul was talking about just the opposite. He was describing "that which has the dignity of holiness upon it." The thoughts of the Christian are not to be set on ways of pleasure, or the easy ways and things of life. It is all right to have genuine regard for comfort, but comfort and ease and pleasure are not to be the principal things. The Christian's thoughts are to have to do, primarily, with his response to duty—duty to God and duty to man.

Third, the mind of the Christian is to dwell upon things that are *just*. The word Paul used for "just" is *dikaios*. The Greeks regarded the *dikaios* man (the man who is righteous) as one "who gives to gods and men that which is their due."[4] The *dikaios* (just person) is a person who has faced his duty and performed it.

It is easy for the followers of Christ to choose the pathway that is pleasant and marked by comfort, but God expects them to respond to life in the light of their duty both to God and to persons. What seems pleasant at the moment may become bitter at the end. And that which may appear difficult and painful in the beginning may be full of joyful rewards at the end.

Fourth, the thoughts of the Christian are to dwell upon things that are *pure*. The word translated *pure (hagna)* is an old word that was used in Paul's day for all kinds of purity. It referred to clean things, clean thoughts, clean words, clean deeds.

The basic idea in the word *hagnos,* as here used, describes that which is "morally pure, that which is undefiled." When used ceremonially, as in acts of Temple worship, it portrayed a thing as having been cleansed and made suitable both for God's presence and service.

Today's world is full of soiled and dirty things—things that are base and shameful to name, much less think about. The media, for instance, is so contaminated with profane words and profane thinking that it is necessary to monitor programs and reading matter where children are involved. Actually the monitoring is necessary for adults, also, if one does not want his mind to slip into a state of such impurity that it tends to contaminate everything it touches. The thoughts of the Christian are to be clean thoughts, pure thoughts, thoughts that will pass not only the scrutiny of people but of God.

When persons allow their minds to become contaminated with the things that are impure, they lose the ability to distinguish between that which is right and that which is wrong. The fine, cutting edge of the knife of conscience becomes dull and the spiritual eye dim. It was of this that the prophet Isaiah spoke, saying, "Woe unto them that call evil good, and good evil; that put darkness for light, and light for darkness; that put bitter for sweet, and sweet for bitter!" (5:20).

Fifth, he who would have the peace of God must also set his mind on the things that are *lovely*. The word *lovely* comes from an old word used only here in the New Testatment, and is derived from two words (*pros* and *phileo*) meaning "pleasing, winsome." Perhaps the translation might well read, "Whatever things are winsome," or elicit love on the part of others.

This is the opposite state of mind to that which deals in bitterness and fear in relation to others. Those who deal with rebuke and thrive on thoughts of vengeance and punishment elicit only bitterness, resentment, and retaliation in return.

The Christian is to be a winsome person, and to achieve this quality of character his mind must be set on lovely things. Love, mercy, sympathy, forbearance, and a spirit of helpfulness must ever mark his life-style. The way to have a friend is to be one. And the Christian ought to be such a friend, in thoughts and in deeds, that to see him is to love him!

Step 6

Sixth, the one who is on the quest for peace is also to set his mind on the things that are *of good report*. The word Paul used is an old word *(euphema),* used only here in the New Testament, and means "fair-speaking, attractive." In the margin of the Revised Standard Version one finds the word *gracious*. Moffatt has *high-toned*. The American Standard Version has *gracious*.

So much conversation today is sprinkled with words that are impure and false. Such words are not to fall from the lips of the Christian. In truth, if the mind of the Christian is set on things that are pure, he will hardly speak words that are not of good report. His words will always be words that are fit for God to hear.

Paul rounded out his words of admonition concerning the set of the minds of the followers of Jesus by saying, "If there be any virtue, and if there be any praise, think on these things" (v. 8). Both the American Standard Version and Moffatt used the word *excellence* rather than *virtue*. The word translated *virtue* is an old word *(arete)* which may come from the word *aresko* meaning "to please." It is widely used "in a variety of senses by the ancients for any mental excellence or moral quality or physical power."[5]

In classical usage, the word *arete* could describe "the excellence of the ground in a field, the excellence of a tool for its purpose, the physical excellence of an animal, the excellence of the courage of a soldier, and the virtue of a man."[6] The word is rarely used in the New Testament, but it is in common usage in the papyri. Some think that Paul's use of the term may be in the sense found in the Septuagint (LXX) translation of the Old Testament (in Isa. 42:12; 43:21) where there is a tone of praise that reflects the splendor and might of God.

Paul's entreaty to "think on these things" means in the verb form (present middle imperative) that the follower of Christ is *to have the habit* of thinking "on these things." It is not to be a passing thing but a continuing mood and disposition of thought. After all, a man can control his thoughts if he is disposed to do so and is willing to discipline himself accordingly. He may not be able to keep the wrong kind of thoughts from entering his mind occasionally, but he is certainly able to keep them from finding a resting place in his mind and heart. One has to make a choice in the world he faces. He will choose to think about the degradations, the impurities, and the immoral relations of life, or else he will set his mind to think on "its nobilities and its chivalries," on its virtues in every realm.

As to Paul's words "if there be any praise," he was not saying that a good man is not to be moved "and uplifted by the praise of good men"—not that; rather he was saying that a person is to live in such a way that the praise of good men is neither to become the occasion of conceit nor unholy desire.

EXERCISE

Take your Bible, return to your quiet place of prayer and meditation and read again and again the passage which I have just discussed. With this book open before you, meditate upon Paul's words. Contemplate afresh, one by one, the "whatever things" that he has called upon the followers of Jesus to set their minds on.

Ask yourself these questions: What is the life-style of my mind? Am I given to thinking upon the kind of things of which Paul has spoken in verse 8? Do I find in them my chief delight, or rather, is my mind given to "feasting" upon the opposite? How pure are my thoughts as I mingle with other people and look upon them? How just are my evaluations of others? How lovely are my thoughts and to what extent are my words of good report?

What do I read first in the newspaper: The things that are

Step 6

lovely and of good report, or do I turn first to the stories that have to do with things that are unlovely?

What do I share most in my conversation with others—the things that are true, honest, just, pure, lovely, of good report—or do I share the opposite kind of things?

Are my thoughts such as I would want to pass in review before the mind of God? Do I have a thought life-style that will answer favorably to Paul's admonitions in Philippians 4:8?

Am I satisfied with my life-style of thought? Are there points at which I should effect a change?

Then kneel and pray this prayer (or a prayer of your own wording): "Dear Heavenly Father, help me to take to heart the holy admonition of thy words which I have dwelt upon today. Give me the ability, I pray, to distinguish between the things that differ and help me to be able to apply that difference in my own way of thinking and living. Help me to develop a thought style that is in keeping with thy precepts, I pray. And when I have begun to develop, more effectively, that thought style, help me to see the difference. In Jesus' name. Amen."

Step 7
Practice the Gospel

What you have learned and accepted and heard and seen in me, these things continue to practice (Phil. 4:9b).

It is one thing to have knowledge, to know what is best to do, but it is an altogether different thing to put that knowledge into practice. What good is to be realized if one knows perfectly the words of the apostle Paul that we have dealt with, step by step in the quest for peace, and does not endeavor to put these truths into practice? "What you have learned and accepted and heard and seen in me," said Paul, "these things continue to practice, and the God of the peace shall be with you" (v. 9).

Suppose a loved one is gravely ill, and the physician has made his diagnosis, laid out the medicine to be applied, and given full instruction on procedures. What is to be gained if the directions are not followed and the medicine is left lying on the bedside table?

So it is with many of us who have distracted minds and troubled hearts. It is not that we are unaware of at least some of the things we ought to do . . . some of the courses of action we ought to take, but we do not seem to have the disposition and the presence of mind to take the course that is best.

Even so, Paul came to the heart of the quest for peace in verse 9 when he entreated his Philippian friends to *practice* what they had *learned* and *accepted*. The things learned, of which Paul spoke, refer to his personal instruction—relating to the gospel and its teachings as he brought it to them. Paul literally laid bare the intimate thoughts of his soul as he shared with the Philippians the great doctrines of the faith as he himself had come to understand them and to put them into practice. He did not bring to them the words of a neophyte, a beginner only recently planted in the way of God; he spoke as a battle-scarred veteran of the Word and of the way of the Lord. He spoke as a man of both faith and works. And what he was really saying was this: "Imitate my example . . . do as I have done!"

Paul did not claim to be a sinless man. He knew well enough that only God is without sin. But he did know that he had put his whole soul, his whole life, into the striving for the peace and the way of Christ, and he had learned much on the pilgrimage.

Paul laid everything he had on the line for Jesus, and that without regret. Hear him as he told of his experience in Christ: "But whatever things were gains to me, these I have deliberately regarded as loss because of Christ. Yea rather indeed I still consider all things to be loss because of the surpassing greatness of the personal knowledge of Christ Jesus my Lord, for whose sake I suffered the loss of all things, and regard them as rubbish in order that I might gain Christ, and be found in him, not having my own righteousness that is of the law, but the righteousness that is through faith in Christ, the righteousness of God that is based on the faith" (Phil. 3:7-9).

The word *received,* as Paul used it here, refers to the acceptance of a "fixed tradition"—in this case the doctrine and truth of the Christian premise concerning the church and the individual believer as set forth in the written Word of God and accepted by the churches. But true teaching consists of more than the mere sharing of a given body of truth or doctrine. In sharing the premise, one must illuminate it by means of his own personal interpretation and instruction. We sometimes refer to this as "preaching through personality." The witness himself must first be indoctrinated in the message. He must know it thoroughly, backwards and forwards; then letting his own mind serve as a sieve, he separates the principal thing and passes it on to others.

Few teachers can say to their students what Paul said in effect to his Philippian friends, "Copy me; do as I have done. Put into practice the truths that I have come to experience myself and to share with you." Every Philippian knew that Paul, as a teacher, had done just that; he had already put into practice his words to them.

It is at this point that we come to one of our chief weaknesses as followers of Christ. We simply do not strive faithfully enough to practice the truths we have learned. "In theory," said Epictetus, "there is nothing to hinder our following what we are taught; but in life there are many things to draw us aside."[1]

Christianity is not a garment to be worn and laid aside at the whim of circumstance. The mission of Christ's follower is to be as constant as one's days. Jesus said, "I am the way, and the truth, and the life" (John 14:6), and this means that his followers are to seek to imitate his life-style in all their ways.

"Were I a nightingale," said Epictetus, "I would act the part of a nightingale; were I a swan, the part of a swan."[2] And "practice," said Publius Syrus (Maxim 439) "is everything." Whether or not we agree with this maxim, we know that we are to be "doers of the word, and not hearers only" (Jas. 1:22), deceiving ourselves; for "faith apart from works is barren" (2:20), and "What doth it profit, my brethren, if a man say he hath faith, but have not works?" (2:14).

Many of us who profess to be followers of Christ act as though we do not know him at all; for to know him truly is to accept him as "the way, the truth, and the life," and to strive earnestly to keep his commands in all our ways.

In truth, many of us act as little children, for what is the true difference between a child and a full-grown person save that in the case of the child there is a lack of instruction, whereas the full-grown person is fully informed? The child has the capacity for knowledge just as the adult, but the child cannot be expected to put into practice the ways of the adult for the simple reason that the child lacks the knowledge and the motivation to do so.

Perhaps the saddest words ever spoken by Jesus to his disciples were these: "I have yet many things to say unto you, but ye cannot bear them now" (John 16:12). Think what it would have meant to the waiting world had Jesus been able to speak all the thoughts of his mind and heart to his disciples. But doubtless some of them would have turned away just as did the multitudes by the sea of Galilee who, stung by the words of Jesus and faulty in their understanding, said, as they turned away, "This is a hard saying; who can hear it?" (John 6:60).

Likewise, the saddest words ever spoken by Paul to his fellow Christians, I suppose, were these: "And I, brethren, could not speak unto you as unto spiritual, but as unto carnal, as unto babes in Christ. I fed you with milk, not with meat; for ye were not yet able to bear it: nay, not even now are ye able; for ye are yet carnal" (1 Cor. 3:1-3).

It all boils down to this: Do we really desire peace, God's peace? If we desire it, then there is a price to pay. The peace of God does not come in a willy-nilly manner. There can be no vacillating, no shilly-shallying. The Christian is not to dwell in the mood of irresolution, ambivalence, and indecision. A disciple is to be a person of outer action as well as of inner faith.

True is the ancient proverb, "Practice makes perfect," and this is seen in a very beautiful way in the growth and development of the little child. Well do I remember the birth of our first

Step 7

grandchild. When we brought her for the first time to the table, sat her in her own high chair, and gave her a bowl of pabulum and a little silver spoon, all her own, with which to eat by herself, I recall how awkward she was, how clumsy in every move of her tiny little hands as she grasped the spoon. I can see her now as she played with the spoon, dipped it in the pabulum, and now and then lifted a portion of it toward her mouth (usually it landed on the side of her cheek). What is more, I noticed that almost as much of the pabulum went to the floor below as to her little waiting mouth! And as I looked at the floor where the fallen food lay on the beautiful rose-colored Chinese rug, I wondered if the rug would ever come clean again! Then I thought of the words of Chaucer in his "Canterbury Tales" and of the delicate sense of refinement with which the cultured lady lifted the cup to her lips and drank, without leaving even the slightest smudge from her lips on the rim of the cup, and I said to myself, *One day she will be like that; it will only take instruction and practice!*

But growth and development come through practice, for practice is the twin sister of development and growth. All development in the moral realm calls for discipline of mind and heart and hand. There is forever the struggle on the part of the disciplined person in the quest for the full enjoyment of the ways of God. Even Paul said:

> For I know that in me, that is, in my flesh, dwelleth no good thing: for to will is present with me, but to do that which is good is not. For the good which I would I do not: but the evil which I would not, that I practise. But if what I would not, that I do, it is no more I that do it, but sin which dwelleth in me. I find then the law, that, to me who would do good, evil is present. For I delight in the law of God after the inward man: but I see a different law in my members, warring against the law of my mind, and bringing me into captivity under the law of sin which is in my members (Rom. 7:18-23).

Often in counseling with young couples before marriage, I

discuss with them the matter of how they are to spend their days together and apart as they engage in the tasks of life that confront them. And frequently I say to them, "Make it the habit of your life to think good thoughts. Set your mind on things that are beautiful and uplifting. If possible, try to listen to some beautiful music each day. Cultivate the habit of reading something beautiful and uplifting daily. Seek to meet the needs of your partner rather than expecting to have your needs met.

A pastor recalls the first time he attempted to stand on his feet before an audience and speak a good word for Jesus. Said he,

> Frankly, I was frightened half to death. When I rose to my feet, I was not even sure that I could stand, for my knees were so wobbly! I was wearing, at the time, a gray pair of trousers that were "bell-bottomed," being fashioned somewhat after a sailor's trousers. I said when the experience was over, "Now I know why they make bell-bottom trousers; they make them to hide the knocking knees of young people who have to get up before a crowd and make a talk!" (But all of that fear and embarrassment has passed away. Now I have no sense of fear or timidity as I stand before an audience. Practice has done away with all of that—and I might add, Thank the Lord!)

Paul was saying in substance, "Now you know something of the quest for peace: It is a journey, a pilgrimage; come along and get with it! You are a pilgrim, and you are going somewhere. Put these steps into practice. Let them become part and parcel of your daily life. Dwell with them in your inmost thoughts as you would pleasantly dwell with the memory of the happy experiences you have had in life."

In the words of Rowland Howard,

> . . . Let your watchword be dispatch, and practise what you preach;
> Do not let your chances like sunbeams pass you by,
> For you never miss the water till the well runs dry.[3]

Last of all, Paul reminded his Philippian friends if they would discipline themselves and be faithful in the practice of the teachings that he had left them, if they would demonstrate "in action" the instruction which he had endeavored to put in words, and do this faithfully, the peace of God would be with them! "What you have learned and accepted and heard and seen in me, these things continue to practice, and the God of the peace shall be with you" (v. 9). He even went so far as to say, "And the peace of God, which surpasses all understanding shall guard your hearts and your thoughts with Christ Jesus."

EXERCISE

Go apart, to your place of prayer, and sit down in the quiet of your solitude and read again these words of Paul, seeking to read them earnestly and with understanding.

In your meditation, try to let your whole life unfold before you, as a vast panorama, starting with your childhood, and coming all the way to the present. Allow your much-varied and multicolored experiences to pass before you in kaleidoscopic review.

Endeavor to discern to what extent you have put into practice, in the various life situations that have confronted you, such knowledge, such Christian teachings, as you have known. Have you lived a life of discipline in the Christian tradition? Or have you allowed your life to go by in a happy-go-lucky manner—without serious thought, without seasons of meditation, reflection, and self-inquiry in the light of God's words?

Think of the lives of some of the noble Christians you have known, and lay your life down alongside theirs and contemplate the difference. Try to determine the basis of the difference, the cause.

When you have done this, kneel prayerfully and wait on the Lord. Listen for his voice—the intimations that come to your mind as you wait in silence.

After he has spoken to you, speak to him the intimate thoughts of your heart. Speak as you would to your own mother, were you a little child longing for her understanding.

Speak gently, quietly, and vocalize your thoughts, your hopes, your dreams for peace. Tell the Father of your love for him and for his Son, our Savior, and for his way of life. Then resolve that henceforth, with his help, you will think on the things you have received and heard from his Word, and endeavor to practice them as you daily go your way, in ways that others as well as God will know.

And remember:

> There is a saying of the ancient sages:
> No noble human thought,
> However buried in the dust of ages,
> Can ever come to naught.[4]

God's Peace

And the God of the peace shall be with you (Phil. 4:9b).

Any serious study of the seven steps to peace, as the apostle Paul outlined them in Philippians 4:4-9, would be incomplete without concluding thoughts about the character of the pilgrims and the pilgrimage of those on the quest for peace. Who are the pilgrims? How do they begin the quest? Is there a prerequisite for those who would follow the guidelines of the apostle Paul? Were his words directed to a special people under God, or to people in general? Is any person able, by his own volition, to pursue this quest effectively? Can he make the journey alone?

Paul's words *were* addressed to a particular people—to Christians of the Philippian church. In the opening verse of the first chapter, he made it clear that his words were directed to "the saints in Christ Jesus" who were in Philippi "together with the bishops and deacons." But who were the "saints," you say?

Basically the word *saint* (Gr. *hagios*) is "used in the New Testament of those whose lives are set apart for or unto God, to be exclusively his."[1] The Philippians were members of the church at Philippi. They were a people who had come to know Jesus as Savior and Lord. Paul regarded them as his brothers in Christ, and every remembrance of them called forth thanksgiving in his heart for their partnership in the gospel "from the first day until the present." They had been his joint partners of the grace both in his bonds "and in the defense and confirmation of the gospel" (1:7).

The Philippians were people who had already begun the Christian pilgrimage. Already they were well along the way, but, like the apostle Paul, they had not yet achieved Christian maturity. There were yet things they could do to aid themselves in their growth and strengthen themselves in their Christian life-style, bringing joy to their hearts in their quest for God's peace. In speaking of his own progress, Paul said, "Not that I already attained or have already been perfected, but I keep pressing on if I also may lay hold of that for which also I was laid hold of by Christ Jesus. Brethren, I do not yet consider to have attained; but one thing I do, forgetting the things that are behind and stretching myself forward towards the things ahead, I keep pressing on toward the goal for the prize of the upward calling of God in Christ Jesus" (Phil. 3:12-14).

Paul loved to think and speak of God as a God of peace. In his introduction to the Book of Romans he concluded by saying, "To all that are in Rome, beloved of God, called to be saints: Grace to you and peace from God our Father and the Lord Jesus Christ" (1:7). "For God is not a God of confusion," said Paul, "but of peace" (1 Cor. 14:33). And in 1 Thessalonians 5:23, he said, "And the God of peace himself sanctify you wholly; and may your spirit and soul and body be preserved entire, without blame at the coming of our Lord Jesus Christ."

In Philippians 4:4-9, therefore, one comes to the heart (the real thrust) of Paul's concept of God's peace. This is why he entreated the Philippians to keep a joyful heart, to manifest reasonableness, to be conscious of the Lord's presence, to avoid overanxiety, to be prayerful, to think good thoughts, and to practice the gospel. These seven steps serve to help deliver the Christian from overwhelming frustrations, doubts,

God's Peace

and bewildering despair so common to those who live apart from God. What is more, such steps lead to the sure and certain peace of God.

Hear Paul's words again: "What you have learned and accepted and heard and seen in me, these things continue to practice, and the God of the peace shall be with you." And again in verse 7: "And the peace of God, which surpasses all understanding shall guard your hearts and your thoughts with Christ Jesus."

But one may ask, "What is the peace of God? What is its character? How is it achieved?"

Certainly, God's peace to the ancient Jew was not looked upon as a negative thing. To him it meant not the absence of trouble. Peace to him included all things that contribute to a person's best estate.

The peace of God does not depend upon material circumstances. It does not derive from the ways of human beings—whether good or bad. God's peace springs from the glad consciousness of a viable and abiding relationship with God the Father through Christ the Son. In a word, it is that blessed state of mind and heart (at times all but detached from pure circumstance) that stems from the Christian's right relationship with both God and man, and from a sincere resolve to know and to do God's will. Such peace leads to the fulfillment of life's best hopes and makes for the noblest fellowship both with God and man. "Thou wilt keep him in perfect peace," said Isaiah, "whose mind is stayed on thee; because he trusteth in thee" (26:3). And again the prophet added, "Trust ye in Jehovah for ever; for in Jehovah, even Jehovah, is an everlasting rock" (v. 4).

This peace is not to be gained by the raw, willful effort of people. Such peace is the gift of God. Human beings themselves are not makers of peace. God's peace is not brought about by human endeavor. This truth is pointed out clearly in chapter 5, verse 1, of Paul's letter to the Romans: "Being therefore justified by faith, we have peace with God through our Lord Jesus Christ." The translators (and commentators) of this verse of Scripture have experienced difficulty with the passage. This is due to the fact that some of the manuscripts have the present active indicative *(echomen)* and translate the passage "we have peace with God." In fact, the Revised Standard Version has "Therefore, since we are justified by faith, we have peace with God through our Lord Jesus Christ." But Westcott and Hort have *echōmen,* present active subjunctive mode which is "volitive," and means rather, "*Let us have* peace with God."[2] By following the text of Westcott and Hort, one arrives at an altogether different meaning. The words *being justified* (first aorist passive participle) mean "being set right with God" and express "antecedent action with the words *let us have peace.*" The word *therefore* (that is, "being justified therefore") harks back to the arguments of chapters 1-4 and should make it clear to all that man's justification by God springs out of the realm of faith.

And although the peace of which Paul spoke does not depend upon material circumstances, or any external force or human relationship, there are many Christians who do not seem to have this peace as a continuing experience. Of this obvious fact every Christian counselor is surely aware. Ask any professing Christian this question: "Do you always have in your mind and heart the peace of which Paul spoke in Philippians 4:7 and 9? Or, are there times in your life when the flow of the river of peace is at an extremely low ebb with little or no flow at all?" You will likely have an answer that runs like this: "No, not always. There are times when my heart is quiet and untroubled. At other times, I seem to have no peace at all."

Paul's words in Romans 5:1 ff. make it clear that peace in the heart of the Christian may be unfailing instead of a wavering, faltering estate. This is because the basis of peace is estab-

God's Peace

lished by God and not by man. "My peace I give unto you," said Jesus (John 14:27). "Being justified therefore . . . ," said Paul, "let us keep on having peace with God through our Lord Jesus Christ" (Rom. 5:1, author's translation).

God's peace is not something that man achieves by himself. He never has. He never will. And the seven steps to peace are only an exercise of faith designed to make more real that which has already been made possible for the believer through the activity of God who delivered him from wrong into right and started him on the pilgrimage.

Peace in the heart of man is possible because of a new relationship that exists between him and God—a relationship in which he has been born "from above" and entered into the Christian life-style. This new estate, made possible by justification, is antecedent to peace. Without it there can be no peace. With it there can be peace forever.

The foundation of peace, God's peace, was laid by God and not by human beings. Mankind is mortal, sinful, and without the capacity to lay the broad, deep foundation for the structure of peace in the human heart. Mankind is of a sinful disposition and has a heart that is "deceitful above all things," said Jeremiah, "and it is exceedingly corrupt" (17:9). And this corruption, by nature, extends to all people since "all have sinned, and fall short of the glory of God" (Rom. 3:23).

Peace is made possible by the Justifier who is the Lord of creation, the God of all being. As Paul said (Rom. 3:24 *ff.*), Christians have already been "justified freely by his grace through the redemption that is in Christ Jesus: whom God set forth to be a propitiation, through faith, in his blood." And this, he added, was "to show his righteousness because of the passing over of the sins done aforetime, in the forbearance of God; for the showing, I say, of his righteousness at this present season: that he might himself be just, and the justifier of him that hath faith in Jesus" (Rom. 3:25-26).

Here we come to a basic fallacy in human reasoning, a fallacy which lies at the heart of humanistic, materialistic philosophy. This fallacy becomes evident in the testimony of Whittaker Chambers, a former Communist who was quoted widely following his defection from Communism. He described Communism, in substance, as a "semimilitant faith" in which people acknowledge no reliance upon God for either wisdom, guidance, or strength. It is a philosophy whereby people endeavor to lift themselves up out of the miry clay of human circumstance by their own technology and strength, as they tug at their own boot straps. It is the only crusade in history, said Chambers, where the crusader does not look up to God for guidance and support. This fact is vividly illustrated in an experience I had in Stalingrad, Russia, the city that was so completely devastated when the German army under General Von Paulus and the Russian forces under General Chukov met in deadly encounter.

Upon visiting a kindergarten in Stalingrad, I saw on the walls of the kindergarten a printed schedule of the daily activities and observed that in the routine of the procedural care of the little ones there was no reference to God—no activity that had to do with the things of the Spirit.

Structurally, the kindergarten appeared to be well designed. Spotless sheets were on the beds. The floors and the walls were clean. The playthings were nice in appearance and well kept. And the children themselves appeared to be robust and healthy, as any child should be.

The kindergarten director and her assistants were dressed in spotless white garments and seemed to move about responsibly and kindly in their efforts to care for the children and to direct them in their activities.

Upon seeing no reference to any spiritual activity in a schedule that was carefully outlined from beginning to end, I remarked to the director, "But I see, in your daily routine, no

God's Peace

reference to God or to things of the Spirit!"

"We do not use that word here," she curtly replied.

Like Communists, people in general must feel that there is little need for this act of justification on the part of God whereby the only foundation for peace in the heart (and in the world at large) is laid. They appear rather to seek peace in their own way, by their own method, as they pursue their own goals.

But peace is not realized in this way. Only God can prepare the heart of a person for the peaceful pilgrimage, and this is done by his act of justification whereby he enables the person to move from the debit side of the spiritual ledger to the credit side. It is God who enables the person to pass from darkness unto light, from death unto life!

There is a word much used in medical language called *etiology*. The word comes from middle Latin *(aetiologia)* which in turn comes from the Greek word *aitiologia,* from *aitia* meaning *cause.* So etiology, in medicine, has to do with the cause or origin of a disease or abnormal condition. Even so, the etiology of peace in the heart of a person springs from God's love for the world (John 3:16) and his providential act of justification of those who are convicted of their sins (their abnormal relationship to God and the world about them, their transgression of divine law) and who seek his forgiveness and loving care. The apostle Paul, whose brilliant mind was perhaps without a peer among the followers of Christ, expressed the basis for this peace relationship clearly: "Being therefore justified by faith," he said, "let us keep on having peace."

Now the meaning of the words *by faith (ek pisteōs)* is made clear by Paul's use of the preposition *by (ek)* which always has the meaning *out of,* a meaning that "never varies."[3] The words mean that the activity by which God "sets man right" springs out of the realm of faith. Man does not bring this act of justification about, but he does cooperate with God in his effort to effect deliverance from sin by exercising faith.

And what is faith? Faith is "Belief, trust; the leaning of the entire self upon God or Messiah in absolute trust and confidence for his salvation, wisdom, guidance, strength."[4]

Without faith, there can be no justification, no foundation for the steps to peace. Nor can the steps to peace be taken by the believer without faith. Paul stated the matter clearly in his letter to the Ephesians: "For by the grace you have been saved through faith; and that not out of you: it is the gift of God; not of works, so that no one may boast" (2:8-9). Likewise, in Romans 5:1 *ff*. Paul pointed out that the instrument or channel by which this glorious transaction is achieved is our Lord Jesus Christ, for it was through him "also we have had our access by faith into this grace wherein we stand."

The word *access (prosagōgē)* suggests an *entree* "or perhaps a metaphor from the concrete sense *landing-stage*."[5] In other words, it is through Christ that man has the beachhead, or the landing stage, for the Christian pilgrimage which begins with the act of justification—the deliverance from sin which was made possible by the loving heart of God. And while this act of justification was accomplished by God, it was the Lord Jesus Christ who became for him the instrument whereby the transaction was made. Moreover, it is Christ, as the writer of Hebrews tells us (12:2), who is "the author and perfecter of our faith, who for the joy that was set before him endured the cross, despising shame, and hath sat down at the right hand of the throne of God."

Paul's words "access by faith into this grace wherein we stand" suggest the metaphor of a *field,* or *area,* or *new world of faith and works.*

The word *grace* which Paul used in Romans 5:2 *(charin)* is a word that in early Greek literature had variant meanings of *gracefulness, gratitude, favor*. Here the idea seems to be that of a *"lovely, unmerited, God-given experience* of his favoring presence felt in the life of man. Peace comes only to those who have first received grace."[6] And the grace, in this instance (Rom. 5:2), is made possible by God's act of delivering (5:1) the sinner from his old life-style into a new lifestyle that is in accord with the way, the truth, and the life of Jesus. Wherever the Christian moves in the world about him, he is surrounded by God's favoring presence. It should be noted that Paul's words (Rom. 5:1) make it clear that the peace of which he spoke is peace "with God" *(pros ton Theon).*

The reason man continues to be plagued by wars and rumors of wars is due to the fact that men do not have "peace with God." For, as Jacques Maretain, the French philosopher, aptly expressed it, if we would change the face of the world we must first change our own hearts.

Still, it is a sad mistake to think of peace, God's peace, as a condition that never wears the garments of trouble. Troubles may come, and troubles may go, but the peace of God goes on forever in the hearts of those who know the Heavenly Father and who seek constantly to stand in right relationship with him and with their fellowmen.

The character of this peace of which Paul spoke, God's peace, surpasses all human understanding. It is past tracing out! No one can delineate fully the height, the length, the breadth, and the depth of God's peace. It is a peace that springs from God—that issues from his throne of mercy and belongs to him. It does not come from the devices of people. It is not something gained by earthly powers. It is not the result of the cessation of the hostilities of war—whether of nations or of individuals. It consists of an inner quality of mind and heart that is of the character of God himself. That is why God's peace is marked by hope. "Now the God of hope fill you with all joy and peace in believing, that ye may abound in hope, in the power of the Holy Spirit" (Rom. 15:13).

The ways of God are eternal. They never pass away. His commands, his laws, his designs for mankind are inexorable. They yield not to the schemes of human beings. They change not. "For verily I say unto you," said Jesus, "Till heaven and earth pass away, one jot or one tittle shall in no wise pass away from the law, till all things be accomplished" (Matt. 5:18).

For one who believes in God, and trusts in him with all his heart, there is no such thing as ultimate despair. The perfidies of humanity, the hatreds, the insults, the vituperative flailings of the human tongue, the insulting injuries of interpersonal human relationships, even all these cannot plunge the child of God into despair when the mind is stayed on God.

God's providence is overruling. And it is the consciousness of this overriding destiny of the children of God that keeps one from despair. Well might the psalmist say,/"Why art thou cast down, O my soul?/And why art thou disquieted within me?/Hope thou in God; for I shall yet praise him/For the help of his countenance" (42:5).

In the words of F. W. Faber,

> For right is right, since God is God,
> And right the day must win;
> To doubt would be disloyalty,
> To falter would be sin.[7]

As believers continue in fellowship with God, advance in understanding of Christian truth and in the knowledge of what God is and of what God is like, little by little they take on something of the character of God. They take on patience, for God is a God of patience; they experience comfort, for God is a comforting presence; they have consolation in their hearts, for God is a God of consolation. "Now the God of patience and of comfort grant you to be of the same mind one with another," said Paul, "according to Christ Jesus: that with one accord ye may with one mouth glorify the God and Father of

God's Peace

our Lord Jesus Christ" (Rom. 15:5-6).

The story is told of a traveler who came across a piece of clay that was redolent with perfume. Gripped by the mystery of it, the traveler spoke to the piece of clay, asking how it came to be thus; to which the piece of clay replied, "Stranger, if the secret I must disclose, I have been dwelling with a rose."

So it is with those who dwell in sweet fellowship with the Father through Christ our Lord. Little by little, more and more, the individual comes to be like him.

What is more, eventually the heart of the believer begins to overflow with love, for God is the God of love and peace, even as Paul said in his farewell words to his friends of Corinth, "Be perfected; be comforted; be of the same mind; live in peace: and the God of love and peace shall be with you" (2 Cor. 13:11).

God the Father is, said Paul, "the Father of mercies and God of all comfort; who comforteth us in all our affliction, that we may be able to comfort them that are in any affliction, through the comfort wherewith we ourselves are comforted of God. For as the sufferings of Christ abound unto us, even so our comfort also aboundeth through Christ" (2 Cor. 1:3-6). And let us remember that the word patience, as Paul used it, "never means simply the ability to sit down and bear things; it means to rise up and conquer things. It does not mean simply to accept things; it means to accept them, and to change them into glory."[8]

Marie Monsen, a Norwegian missionary to North China during the time of the great revival there (1927-1937), tells the story of a man of about sixty to seventy years of age who came in one evening and said:

"Many have been saved."
"How do you know that?"
"I can see it in their faces."

"Yes, but you know, these days the Lord looketh on the heart."

"What I see in their faces comes from what has happened in their hearts."

"What has happened in their hearts?"

"Sin has come out and God's peace has gone in."

"How did it happen?"

"They confessed their sins and were given new hearts. I want to confess too," and he knelt down. He prayed a very, very long prayer, a dead prayer.

"Do you call this getting right with God?"

For a few moments he sat in silence, then went away. Next day he was there again.

"I wasn't sincere yesterday."

"I can go out while you speak to the Lord."

And this time it was real . . . He was given peace and his face shone for joy.[9]

Paul tells us in Romans 8:28 that God works with us (who are his called) in all things unto good. He works with us, and he works for us. He helps us to make the best out of the worst that comes our way. We look to him for the way out, and he shows us the way clearly and helps us.

God's comfort and consolation *(paraklesis)* may be realized in soothing sympathy, in a given hour of need, but it amounts to far more than this: It strengthens, encourages, inspires. It is an enabler, giving the believer the ability to face life afresh in spite of life's conflicts and to be confident of victory in the end!

The Christian may have his moments of doubt, but never are his doubts unto despair. He knows that there is a better day ahead. He knows that "There is therefore now no condemnation to them that are in Christ Jesus" (Rom. 8:1). But he also knows "that the sufferings of this present time are not worthy to be compared with the glory which shall be revealed to us-

God's Peace

ward" (Rom. 8:18). Furthermore, the Christian knows that even when his prayers seem to fail him (how often, in counseling with distracted souls, have I heard the echo of that feeling), "the Spirit also helpeth our infirmity: for we know not how to pray as we ought; but the Spirit himself maketh intercession for us with groanings which cannot be uttered; and he that searcheth the hearts knoweth what is the mind of the Spirit, because he maketh intercession for the saints according to the will of God. And we know that to them that love God all things work together for good, even to them that are called according to his purpose" (Rom. 8:26-28).

The peace of God, God's peace, is an active thing, and moves under the initiative of God. This is why Paul said, "And the peace of God which surpasses all understanding shall guard your hearts and your thoughts with Christ Jesus" (Phil. 4:7).

God's peace is not to be a passing thing. It is as lasting as time itself. And it is so great that it defies all understanding!

The King James Version has "shall keep your hearts and your minds through Christ Jesus," but the American Standard Version has "shall guard your hearts and your thoughts in Christ Jesus," which is preferable. The word translated "keep" (Gr. *phrouresei*) is a military term. It has to do with soldiers and literally means to "guard" or "garrison." And this is the figure which I believe Paul meant to leave with his Philippian friends.

Here the concept is that of the believer who is distressed, all but distracted, depressed, and suffering from the fiery darts of the evil one, hardly knowing which way to turn, while out on the edge of things is the person of Satan himself seeking to assail the believer, and to overwhelm him with doubts and despair. But always, said Paul, there is Jesus who stands between the believer and Satan, as a guard, as a garrison of soldiers. In whatever direction Satan moves in his effort to assault the believer, Jesus stands between, fencing off the blows, hurling back the attack. Consequently, Satan can only turn away in bitter defeat, just as he turned from Jesus on the mount of temptation as Jesus said unto him, "Be gone, Satan! For it is written, you shall worship the Lord your God and him only shall you serve" (author's translation). In such an hour, even as with Jesus, angels will come and minister unto the beleaguered one, who will then have peace—God's peace.

This realm of grace, in which we who believe in Christ stand, came to us by faith, and still belongs to us. Paul's use of the words *in which we stand (en hēi hestēkamen)* (Rom. 5:2) is a perfect active indicative verb of *histēmi* in the intransitive form. This means that, with God's help, we have achieved access to this field of grace and it is still ours. Though it happened in the past, it still holds good. And it can be as real for the believer all along the pilgrimage of life as it was in the beginning if he will continue steadfast in the faith and allow the grace of God to operate in his life.

Even so, Paul enjoined the Christian to *keep on* having this peace in his heart. The believer had it in the beginning when he was delivered completely from his sins. But though he was delivered and though he had the peace in the beginning, he does not always experience peace in his heart in a continuing manner. He allows himself to become upset, distressed, and overanxious when he faces the vexing circumstances of life. Such ought not to be, for again, peace of mind and heart is not dependent upon human circumstances, human surroundings. Peace stems from a relationship that exists between the believer and God, a relationship that in spirit and truth is so wonderful in its character that it cannot be described in words. The Christian must always be aware that something better lies ahead. "The sufferings of this present time," said Paul, "are not worthy to be compared with the glory which shall be revealed to us-ward. For the earnest expectation of the creation waiteth for the revealing of the sons of God" (Rom.

8:18-19). Therefore, "Let us exult"[10] *(Kauchōmetha),* said Paul, instead of being downcast. Here again Paul used the present middle subjunctive (volitive), and the emphasis is for the Christian to "keep on enjoying peace with God and keep on exulting in the hope of the glory of God" [Rom. 5:2].[11]

And why not "keep on exulting" since there is "no condemnation to them that are in Christ Jesus" (Rom. 8:1). After all, believers are "not in the flesh," but "in the Spirit, if so be that the Spirit of God" realy dwells in them. What is more, said Paul, "We know that to them that love God all things work together for good, even to them that are called according to his purpose" (Rom. 8:28), and that "in all these things we are more than conquerors through him that loved us" (Rom. 8:37). And all who have put their faith in him, and are born of the Spirit, can stand persuaded "that neither death, nor life, nor angels, nor principalities, nor things present, nor things to come, nor powers, nor height, nor depth, nor any other creature, shall be able to separate us from the love of God, which is in Christ Jesus our Lord" (Rom. 8:38-39).

Notes

Preface
1. R. Paul Caudill, *Philippians: A Translation with Notes* (Boone, NC: Blue Ridge Press of Boone, Inc., 1980). All Scripture quotations from the Book of Philippians are taken from this translation.

Step 1
1. All Scripture quotations other than from the Book of Philippians and the Book of Ephesians are quoted from the American Standard Version of the Bible unless otherwise noted.
2. R. Paul Caudill, *Ephesians: A Translation with Notes* (Nashville: Broadman Press, 1979). All Scripture quotations from the Book of Ephesians are taken from this translation.
3. From "Rabbi Ben Ezra." Stanzas 6, 8, and 12.
4. William Barclay, *The Letters to the Philippians, Colossians, and Thessalonians* (Philadelphia: The Westminster Press, 1959), p. 92.

Step 2
1. James Hope Moulton and George Milligan, *The Vocabulary of the Greek New Testament* (Grand Rapids: Wm. B. Eerdmans Publishing Co., 1949), p. 238.
2. Barclay, p. 93.
3. Ibid., pp. 93-94.
4. *Life*, Vol. I, p. 188.
5. From Henry Wadsworth Longfellow, "The Arrow and the Song."
6. From "Richelieu" (1839), Act I, Scene i.
7. William Barclay, *The Letter to the Hebrews* (Philadelphia: The Westminster Press, 1959), p. 38.
8. Barclay, *The Letters to the Philippians, Colossians, and Thessalonians*, p. 94.

Step 3

1. Caudill, *Philippians,* p. 88.
2. Barclay, *The Letters to the Philippians, Colossians, and Thessalonians,* p. 93.

Step 4

1. Moulton and Milligan, p. 398.
2. Ibid.

Step 5

1. W. Hersey Davis, "Expository Notes on the Gospel of Matthew," written for *The Teacher,* Feb. 2, 1930, pp. 14-15.
2. Ibid.
3. Ibid.
4. From Alfred, Lord Tennyson, *Morte De'Arthur.* Line 415.
5. Barclay, *The Letters to the Philippians, Colossians, and Thessalonians,* p. 95.
6. Ibid., pp. 95-96.
7. Ibid., p. 96.

Step 6

1. Barclay, *The Letters to the Philippians, Colossians, and Thessalonians,* p. 97.
2. A. T. Robertson, *Word Pictures in the New Testament,* Vol. 4 (Nashville: Sunday School Board of the Southern Baptist Convention, 1931), p. 459.
3. Barclay, *The Letters to the Philippians, Colossians, and Thessalonians,* p. 97.
4. Ibid., p. 98.
5. Robertson, p. 460.
6. Deissman, *Bible Studies,* p. 95.

Step 7

1. *Discourses,* chapter 25.
2. Ibid., chapter 16.
3. From *Floruit,* "You Never Miss the Water," Peterson's Magazine, 1876.
4. From John Godfrey Saxe, *Spes est Vates.* Stanza 1.

God's Peace

1. Caudill, *Philippians,* p. 23.
2. Robertson, p. 355.

Notes

3. A. T. Robertson, *A New Short Grammar of the Greek New Testament* (New York: Richard R. Smith, Inc., 1931), p. 256.
4. Caudill, *Ephesians,* p. 25.
5. Alexander Souter, *A Pocket Lexicon to the Greek New Testament* (Oxford: The Clarendon Press, 1943), p. 218.
6. Caudill, *Philippians,* p. 24.
7. From "On the Field" by Frederick William Faber.
8. Barclay, *The Letters to the Philippians, Colossians, and Thessalonians,* p. 102.
9. From *The Awakening,* tr. by Joy Guinness (London: China Inland Mission, 1959), pp. 70-71.
10. Robertson, *Word Pictures,* pp. 355-56.
11. Ibid.

Date Due

Code 4386-04, CLS-4, Broadman Supplies, Nashville, Tenn.,
Printed in U.S.A.